FIGHTING HIGH

WORLD WAR TWO – AIR BATTLE EUROPE

VOLUME TWO

Published in 2010 by Fighting High Ltd,
23 Hitchin Road, Stotfold, Hitchin, Herts, SG5 4HP.
United Kingdom. www.fightinghigh.com

British Library Cataloguing-in-Publication data. A CIP
record for this title is available from the British Library.

ISBN 978 0 9562696 1 4

Designed by Michael Lindley www.truthstudio.co.uk
Aircraft illustrations by Pete West.
Printed and bound by Toppan Printing Co. (UK) Ltd.
Front cover illustration by Steve Teasdale.

FIGHTING HIGH

WORLD WAR TWO – AIR BATTLE EUROPE

VOLUME TWO

COMPILED AND EDITED BY
STEVE DARLOW

CONTENTS

T HE PUBLICATION OF *Fighting High — World War Two — Air Battle Europe, Volume Two* coincides with the seventieth anniversary of one of the most historic and significant battles ever fought in the air, indeed in any military struggle. It has been seven decades since the Royal Air Force won the defensive victory that was the Battle of Britain. With the assistance of airmen from countries allied to Britain, including those who had survived the loss of their homelands to fight another day, these 'Few', as British Prime Minister Winston Churchill called them, met the Luftwaffe head-on, as each opposing air force tried to wrestle the all-important air superiority. The Germans simply had to have command of the air as protection for their invasion forces. The Royal Air Force was not going to give up such an advantage, and a desperate struggle ensued. Combat was ferocious. Death and destruction were ever present. Many who survived, on both sides, suffered physically and psychologically. But their sacrifice secured the postponement of the planned German invasion. Nazi aggression had a new focus in the east. Britain had time and space to recover and respond.

Volume Two begins with the story of the loss of an RAF bomber crew in the Norwegian campaign of April 1940 and one pilot's experiences of the Battle of France, highlighting the value of air superiority in modern warfare. Then some of Fighter Command's heroes tell their story as they prepare for and fight the Battle of Britain. From then on Volume Two tells the story of numerous airmen who took up the fight once British shores had been secured. Britain became an 'aircraft carrier'. Aerial strength was amassed; aircraft were built, shipped or flown in; airfields were constructed; thousands of airmen were trained. Slowly there was a shift from a defensive struggle in Europe to an offensive policy of bombing the enemy and fighting for air superiority over Normandy, France, Belgium, Holland, and the very Reich itself. All this was a result of the platform secured during the Battle of Britain.

Once more it is our pleasure to present the stories of some of the men who fought 'fighting high'. There are tales of tragedy, terrible loss, heroic struggle, and outstanding feats of airmanship. These men come from a generation that will soon be a memory; nevertheless, 'we will remember them'.

Steve Darlow. April 2010

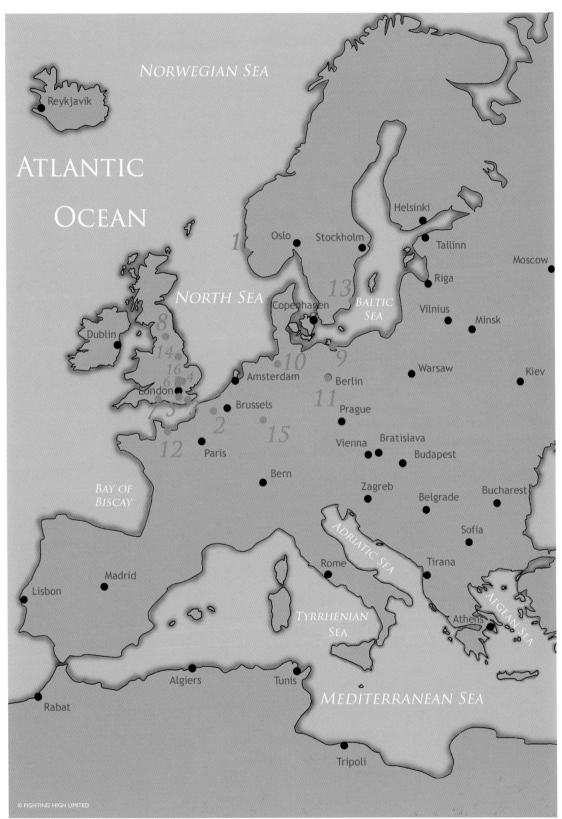

Air Battle Europe

The map shows locations of the stories featured in each chapter of the book

1   Skudeneshavn
2   Lille
3   Hawkinge
4   Duxford and Fowlmere
5   Biggin Hill
6   Kimpton
7   Sturminster Marshall
8   Buckden Pike
9   Peenemünde
10 Albstedt
11 Berlin
12 Bazenville
13 Oland
14 Bardney
15 Bonn
16 Tempsford

EXPOSED AND DEFENCELESS

On 1 April 1940 Adolf Hitler ordered the German armed forces to invade Denmark and Norway, beginning early on the morning of 9 April. He simply had to have Norway under his control. He needed access to the North Sea through Norwegian ports, to secure the supply lines of iron ore from Sweden. The British were similarly aware of the importance of Norway to the German war effort and were keen to keep their enemy away from Norwegian soil. But Hitler's armies overran Denmark and, according to plan and on the day intended, were able to enter the main ports of Norway and seize them with little opposition. Unable to help Denmark, which had offered little opposition and fallen quickly, the Royal Air Force's Bomber Command was ordered to harass and hinder German troop movements in the south of Norway.

Right: Cabinet, holding the Bomber Command Roll of Honour books at Ely Cathedral.

At such range it was impossible for the bombers to have fighter escort. On the first few days of the Norwegian invasion, bomber crews flew hundreds of miles over the sea, trying to find and bomb enemy shipping, and attack airfields captured by the enemy. They had the occasional reported success, but at a price.

On 12 April 1940 Bomber Command carried out what was to be the largest bombing operation of the war to date: 36 Vickers Wellingtons, 24 Handley Page Hampdens, and 23 Bristol Blenheims heading north to attack shipping off the coast of Norway. On arrival at the target area, they encountered determined opposition, both from the ground and in the air. The policy of deploying self-defending daylight bomber formations was put to the test. The resultant losses proved that the policy was flawed. On this day, flying in a Wellington IC of No. 149 Squadron was 23-year-old Aircraftman 2nd Class Harry Gillott and 19-year-old Aircraftman 2nd Class Frederick Tootle. Neither men would survive his encounter with enemy fighters a few miles off the shores of Norway.

From only one of the ten aircraft lost that day were there any survivors: three men from a No. 50 Squadron Hampden survived, although another member of the crew lost his life. A total of forty-four lives were lost on the other aircraft. The majority of their bodies were never discovered, their names now etched into the Air Forces Memorial at Runnymede, Surrey, England, but a few were recovered from the sea. In the days following the raid families were made aware that their sons or husbands were missing. For most, any hopes they held proved in vain. Harry Gillott's body was never found. Freddy Tootle's was recovered, along with that of crewmate Laurie

ANGELA GOOCH

HARRY GILLOTT

Rank: Aircraftman 2nd Class

Unit: 149 Squadron

Date of Death: 12 April 1940

Service No: 623761

Son of Harry and Lavinia Gillott of Sheffield.

Memorial Panel 26: Runnymede Memorial.

Sgt.	Gillis, N. M.	198	17th Dec 1943
AC2.	Gillot, H.	149	12th Apr 1940
Sgt.	Gilman, J. L.	57	19th Aug 1941

Entry in the No. 3 Group Bomber Command Roll of Honour book at Ely Cathedral, Cambridgeshire.

FRED WELLINGS

FREDERICK TOOTLE

Rank: Aircraftman 2nd Class

Unit: 149 Squadron

Date of Death: 12 April 1940

Service No: 625665

Son of John and Grace Tootle of Liverpool

Place of Burial: Falnes Churchyard

Sgt.	Toothill, K. H.	75 Sqn.	15th Sep 1941
AC2.	Tootle, F.	149 Sqn.	12th Apr 1940
P/O.	Toplis, J. G.	214	12th May 1941

Entry in the No. 3 Group Bomber Command Roll of Honour book at Ely Cathedral, Cambridgeshire.

STEVE DARLOW. COURTESY OF ELY CATHEDRAL

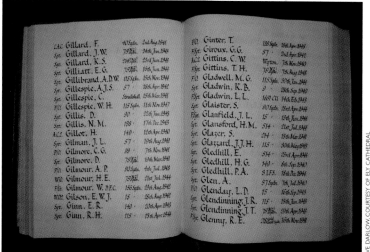

STEVE DARLOW. COURTESY OF ELY CATHEDRAL

Left: No. 3 Group Bomber Command Roll of Honour book at Ely Cathedral, Cambridgeshire, with Harry Gillott's name (sadly misspelt) amid that of other men lost during the war.

Wakeling; both men were buried in Norwegian soil by the Germans.

Still Honoured

Fifty-one years after the event, in 1991, the nephew of Freddy Tootle, another Fred, Fred Wellings, visited Skudeneshavn, on the island of Karmøy, Norway, near where his uncle's Wellington had been shot down. Fred Wellings takes up the story.

I was welcomed by many of the residents, who told me how the graves of Freddy and Laurie Wakeling were still honoured on the Norwegian national day with a graveside ceremony. I was later given the translation of a written account of what had happened, drawn partly from a Norwegian book and partly from memories. The book was Ni dager i april (Nine Days in April) by Knut Mæsel, in which he related a story told to him by a gunner on one of the Wellington bombers in No. 38 Squadron. At 12.30 p.m. they joined with six other Wellingtons from No. 149 Squadron to try to locate the battle cruisers Scharnhorst and Gneisenau. 'It was the first time we had operated with so many aircraft in one mission. Each aircraft had two bombs that were specially constructed to attack warships. They were in fact floating mines, and the idea was to drop them in a circle around the ship…When we reached the Norwegian coast near Stavanger, we saw the snow-covered mountains but we also saw aircraft taking off from an airport under us (Sola). Our intelligence was obviously not well informed, because they had not told us anything about any airport. We did not find the warships we were looking for, and the formation was ordered to split in two. The alarm had gone in Sola airport and the first major air battle was about to start. We were attacked by fighter planes, ten [Me]110s and three Ju88s came up on us from behind, and they managed to shoot down our squadron leader, Noland, and two aircraft from 149 Squadron and one from 9 Squadron.'

After my parents' death, I found the letter written by Freddy's commanding officer, Wing Commander R. Kellett, which added a further perspective. He offered 'more than a faint hope that [Freddy] and his crew may be safe… he was taking part in an operation on Friday afternoon against the enemy, when close alongside the Norwegian coast, the formation was heavily engaged by a number of enemy fighters. His aircraft was hit and forced to go down, but under control, heading for the coast a mile or so away and last seen low on the water. Everyone else was so busily engaged that no one saw whether his aircraft was forced to land on the water or was able to continue to the land. Even if they were forced to land on the water, they had a collapsible boat with which they should have been able to reach the shore.'

FRED WELLINGS

control, heading for the coast a mile or so away and last seen low in the water.

Everyone else was so busily engaged that noone saw whether his aircraft was forced to land on the water or was able to continue to the land.

Even if they were forced to land on the water, they had a collapsible boat with which they should have been able to reach the shore.

It may be sometime before any definite news can get through, and I can well understand what a most anxious period of waiting and hoping this is going to be.

Of course the moment we hear any news at all you will be informed, and we are all praying it will be good news.

Yours sincerely,
R. Kellett.

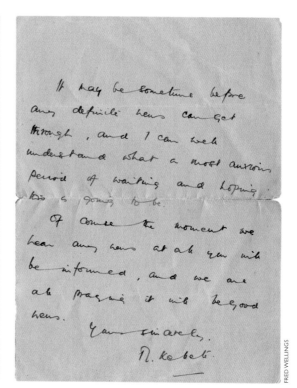

Left: Shortly after Fred Tootle's crew was reported missing, Wing Commander Kellett wrote to Fred's father. At that time there was still hope.

A Rescue Attempt

During Fred Wellings's visit to Skudeneshavn in 1991, he was told that his uncle's aircraft did manage to land on the sea, but with only two of the crew managing to escape. The rest of the story came from a gentleman by the name of Ludvig Thomassen.

Ludwig's father, Sivert, was a ship's pilot and on the morning of 14 April 1940 he had been on duty in the watch tower at Naley. Sivert retained a vivid recollection of that day:

At 0830 we observed an object 2.5 nautical miles off Skardstein rock. The object looked like a small boat. The [ship] pilots gathered and discussed the danger of being attacked by German planes if they investigated the object. We decided to take the risk; there were people in the boat that needed help. Myself, Frithjof Naley, Karl Naley, and Palle Naley went out from Naley pilot station. When we approached the 'boat', we found it to be a dinghy with two British airmen. Both were dead.

They had been injured when they were shot down. One had an injury to his leg and the other to his face. They must have been alive for some time after they climbed into the dinghy because they had eaten their rations. We assumed they had frozen to death. It was a shocking sight, but there was nothing more we could do except take care of the bodies.

We towed the dinghy into more shallow water inside Geitungen, and the bodies were taken on board the pilot vessel. At that time the mayor of Skudeneshavn came aboard and took care of the papers. He handed them over to the Chief of Police and they were identified as Laurie Charles Wakeling and Frederick Tootle. The pilot vessel then honoured the dead by lowering the flag and went into the harbour of Skudeneshavn, where the Red Cross took the bodies to 'Bytunet' [first aid station], where they were taken care of and laid in coffins. The local authority then took

Below left:

Map showing the recovery of the dinghy holding the bodies of Laurie Wakeling and Fred Tootle.

1. Where Sivert Thomassen saw a 'small boat' in the distance.

2. The dinghy in which Laurie Wakeling and Fred Tootle were found.

3. The dinghy is towed back.

4. Where the bodies were retrieved from the dinghy.

5. The route back to Skudeneshavn.

Falnes Churchyard

Skudeneshavn

1
4
5
5
3 Skardstein
Geitungen
2

Right: Fred Wellings at the grave of his uncle, Fred Tootle, in 1991.

over and reported the event to the German commander, who was furious that his own guard force had not seen anything.

The funeral took place two days later, under full military honours at Falnes Churchyard. My father was warned about saying anything at the churchyard, but this was a time of very strong feelings and he therefore placed a bouquet on each coffin and said some words in memory of the two young men who had lost their lives. There were hundreds of people taking part, he told me, and as the coffins were lowered the German soldiers that were present fired shots in the air. From when we were

liberated in 1945, it has been a tradition here in Skudeneshavn to honour those who gave their lives for our freedom on 17 May, our national day. Our own fallen are honoured in the park, and the British airmen are honoured with a ceremony after all the children have paraded to the church.

Terrible News

Fred Tootle's parents, despite the hope offered by Wing Commander Kellet's letter, would eventually have received the terrible news that their son had died. Two other anxious parents were Harry (senior) and Lavinia Gillott, who had also received the awful news

that their son's Wellington bomber had come down over the coast of Norway and that Harry was lost, presumed dead. A few weeks later Harry's younger brother, Leslie, came home from a trip to the local cinema to report that he had seen Harry. Angela Gooch, née Gillott, Leslie's daughter and Harry's niece, takes up the story.

Leslie, who was aged 13 at the time, was watching a matinée at Heeley Picture Palace in Sheffield. The film was a war film showing original news footage and suddenly he saw, flashed on the silver screen, a shot of his brother coming down some aircraft steps then posing with his comrades in front of the bomber. Leslie ran back home to tell his parents, 'Ma, our Harry isn't dead. I've just see him ont' pictures.' She immediately rushed back to the cinema to explain her plight to the manager. The manager produced a still photograph from the cine film and gave it to the distraught mother.

A similar shot from the film appeared in a newspaper and the caption read, 'Here are some of the British pilots who took part in the great aerial battle of Heligoland. Smiles and thumbs up show that they know they had by far the best of it.' The official report of the Heligoland battle stated that 'The laurels go to the Wellington bombers, which resisted the most desperate and, it may be said also, the most courageous and dashing efforts of the enemy's crack fighters to break them up.'

But, of course, as time went by and with no further news coming, Harry was declared missing, presumed dead. His body was never found. In recent years Angela decided to try and trace the actual film that had given her father hope.

Right: The still from the cine film. Harry Gillott is second from the right.

Before Leslie's death in 2001, he had always maintained that the footage of his brother, Harry, was part of a war film. (He was just 13 years old when he saw it!) Despite viewing several war films over the years, including The Lion Has Wings and One of Our Aircraft is Missing, no trace of the footage with Harry in could be found. Then, on 19 April 2005 while browsing the Internet, I found a strong contender for the missing film, Target for Tonight, released in 1941 and directed by Harry Carr. The film had been made with the crew of No. 149 Squadron (no actors) performing their daily routines for the benefit of the camera.

> **"The camera panned to the right and YES! He was there. Harry. And the film actually froze on him at the end. I was elated."**

Harry was in No. 149 Squadron. This film looked like a highly likely candidate. A copy was ordered from a company in Chicago that specialized in war films.

On 23 April 2005, the film was delivered. It wasn't the one. Harry wasn't in it! That same day I launched an appeal for the missing footage on the Internet. The response was tremendous. The Imperial War Museum advised that the still seemed to have been shot at an earlier date than the popular films, suggesting that it could be news footage. A kind helper, via the Internet, provided details of the crew obtained from W. R. Chorley's 'Royal Air Force Bomber Command Losses of the Second World War, Volume 1', and another helper suggested searching the hours of news footage on the Pathé News website. It was also suggested

PICTURES BY TOR SJURSEN

THE CREW OF WELLINGTON IC – P9246 OJ - NO. 149 SQUADRON LOST ON 12 APRIL 1940.

Sergeant Horace J. Wheller – Pilot
(Runnymede Memorial)

Sergeant Laurie C. Wakeling
(Falnes Churchyard)

Sergeant William C. Parker
(Runnymede Memorial)

Leading Aircraftman Richard Coalter
(Runnymede Memorial)

Aircraftman 2nd Class Harry Gillott
(Runnymede Memorial)

Aircraftman 2nd Class Frederick Tootle
(Falnes Churchyard)

that the aircraft in the background was a Wellington, owing to the geodetic fabric and window visible in the background.

A few days later, using the clues various people had given, I typed keywords into the searchable database of Pathé News. Most of the results were immediately discounted because the dates didn't tally. Then I pursued a result that was undated. The description made my heartbeat quicken: 'Air crews disembark from their planes…Group of pilots and crew giving the thumbs up sign.' My thoughts flashed to the newspaper clipping, 'Wellington crew disembarks, gathers on tarmac, thumbs up sign.' I played the preview. Perhaps I recognised the flight sergeant dressed in white flight gear, with a moustache. The camera panned to the right and YES! He was there. Harry. And the film actually froze on him at the end. I was elated. After sixty-five years the footage had been found. But then there was sadness. Those brave, smiling young men didn't realise that three months hence they would be killed!

This archive newsreel brought it home to me exactly what sacrifices were made during the wars, both by the servicemen themselves and the suffering of their families. ∎

(The footage can be viewed on the Pathé News website www.britishpathe.com. Type 'Bombers preparing for take off' into the search field.)

With thanks to Angela Gooch, née Gillott, and Fred Wellings for their help in putting this chapter together. Also Tor Sjursen, Reverend Terje Wallace, Benthe Misje, and Rasmus Ellingsen, who helped with the Norwegian side of the story.

Left: The graves of Fred Tootle and Laurie Wakeling at Falnes Churchyard, on the south-eastern tip of the island of Karmoy, a large island to the north-west of Stavanger. Fred's and Laurie's bodies were recovered from the sea. Many of the locals attended the funeral of the two airmen, at which German soldiers fired a volley in salute of their fallen enemy.

P/O John Greenwood

A Dream Realised

On 10 May 1940 German aggression turned towards France and the Low Countries. In the space of just over a month the German Army punched its way through, or outflanked, any opposition, and the Luftwaffe was able to overwhelm enemy air forces. The Royal Air Force would play its part in the Battle of France, ensuring the attrition rates remained high for both sides. But, as defeat in France became inevitable, the RAF withdrew back across the English Channel, to fight another day. The story of Hawker Hurricane pilot John P. B. Greenwood, as told to **Christopher Yeoman**, records his experiences of the Battle of France and his subsequent involvement in the aerial defence of Britain.

As a small boy John Greenwood used to love reading comics about World War One. Growing up in Kingston, young Greenwood would marvel over the many exciting and intriguing stories about the Tank Corps and the Royal Flying Corps. With such stories catching his youthful imagination, it was there and then that John decided he would quite like to be a fighter pilot if ever there was to be another war. To begin with John considered the idea of being a fighter pilot was something of a pipe dream because his performance at school was lacking – other than on the cricket field:

My results at Tiffin's School, Kingston upon Thames, were of a low standard, as I was only interested in cricket and shooting. I was the youngest member of the first XI at age 14. I also got my colours for shooting. I left school at 14 years 6 months without sitting for either General School or Matriculation. The war clouds were gathering, but my chances of becoming a pilot seemed very slim. However, with the granting of four-and six-year Short Service Commissions, things seemed brighter, and by dint of a few 'white lies' and forging my father's signature, I was summoned for an interview, physical, and psychological tests, which I passed.

Early Days
On 2 February 1939, John Greenwood began his life in the RAF at Perth in Scotland, flying Tiger Moths. His first flight in the two-seater biplane was not as daunting as he had perhaps anticipated. John recalls the trip as being cold and windy, because of the fact that it was midwinter, but overall fairly pleasant. That was, of course, until the

flying instructor decided to introduce John to the world of spins and recoveries.

My instructor showed me an inverted spin, where in the upside-down position he stalled and we spun, but instead of being on the inside of the spin we were on the outside. My body left the seat and my feet the rudder; it was only the straps holding me in! I still remember it as frightening and I can honestly say I have never, ever done one since.

After about eight hours on the Tiger Moth, John went solo. 'I was quite confident and enjoyed it thoroughly. I then had to do three landings and take-offs in quick succession. All went well and no breakages.' In November 1939, John's flying training course at RAF Brize Norton, came to an end, and the students received their various postings. Having also trained on the twin-engine Airspeed Oxford aircraft, which was primarily used to train aircrews in navigation, radio operating, bombing, and gunnery, John fully expected to be sent to a bomber squadron. But to his great surprise and delight he was posted to a fighter unit stationed at RAF Manston in Kent, where he would join No. 253 Squadron.

After being informed that No. 253 Squadron was equipped with Hawker Hurricanes, John's heart sank when he first arrived at the station.

When we arrived at Manston we discovered that our only aircraft were two Miles Magisters. We were forming a brand new squadron, which was originally going to have Bristol Blenheims; this was suddenly changed to a fighter

Opposite page:
Portrait of
John Greenwood.

Right: Battle of France and Battle of Britain pilot John P. B. Greenwood, 1939.

squadron, *as it was decided that they needed five new fighter squadrons and we were one of them. A week later we were equipped with Fairey Battles to practise on, since most of us had been trained on twin engines.*

The Fairey Battle, the single-engine light bomber aircraft, would later be dubbed as 'the flying coffin' by pilots of the time. At the outbreak of war the Fairey Battle was already obsolete. With its slow speed and lack of range, it made an easy target, which subsequently sustained a dreadful casualty rate over France. It was rightly pulled away from the front lines in 1941.

In February 1940, the days of flying Fairey Battles became a thing of the past for the boys of No. 253 Squadron, when two Hawker Hurricanes landed at Manston. 'We were supplied with two Hurricanes from other operational squadrons; of course they were not their best – wooden fix pitch prop, canvas wings and airframe, no bullet proofing or mirrors; but we thought they were terrific.'

Despite the Hurricane being in its early stages of development as a fighter aircraft, the single-seater

JOHN GREENWOOD

monoplane was a vast improvement on anything John had previously flown up until this point. Reflecting upon the early Hurricane MK 1, John remarks:

It was a friendly plane to fly; but take-off seemed long and slow with the fix pitched props. Manoeuvrability was excellent. Most of the pilots had been trained on twins, so we had to find out about aerobatics. I did and enjoyed them thoroughly. However, I never did an outside spin or loop (bunt). By the time we went to France in May, most of us had done between forty and fifty hours.

The Unpleasant Taste of War

Life for John was about to change, when, on 16 May 1940, an Armstrong-Whitworth Ensign aircraft landed at Kenley. The squadron was then told that 'B' Flight (John's flight) was to move all of their belongings into the Ensign, because they were going to France immediately! Shortly after, six aircraft took off for Manston, where they would spend the night until a Blenheim would arrive the following day and lead them to the airfield at Lille Marq in France. On arrival, No. 253 Squadron's 'B' Flight was supposed to join up with No. 111 Squadron, but, as they

Right:
John Greenwood: 'SW-P taken in late April 1940 at Northolt. The next week we returned to Kenley and a few days later, "B" Flight flew to Lille, myself in SW-P.'

JOHN GREENWOOD

were in a totally different part of the airfield, they didn't meet up.

We all slept that night in a tent by our aircraft. We were Flight Lieutenant Anderson, Pilot Officers Clifton, Greenwood, Dawbarn and Corkett, and Sergeant McKenzie. We slept on stretchers. It was freezing cold and we had very little sleep. We had arrived with no commanding officer, adjutant or intelligence officer; they were all back at Kenley. Except for Flight Lieutenant Anderson, who had a two-pitch propeller on his plane, we all had the original Hurricane Mk 1s provided in February, canvas wings and airframes, no armour, no mirrors, and fix pitch wooden props. We flew one sortie that afternoon to patrol Douai and Cambrai, but saw nothing. That night No. 504 Squadron took pity on us, and we slept in the Chateau they occupied. They also fed us, which was the first time we had eaten all day. The aircraft I flew in France was L1712.

Two days later, John got his first unpleasant taste of war. On 18 May 1940, just after dawn, John watched as two Westland Lysanders came in to land at the airfield. Suddenly out of nowhere, four Messerschmitt 109s appeared behind them. 'I was so shocked I heard no gunfire, but watched the two RAF aircraft fly straight into the ground and burst into flames. It was a dreadful introduction to what was ahead.'

Soon after, the air-raid siren wailed across Lille, and John found himself rushing towards his aircraft, with everyone else nearby. In no time at all, every squadron stationed on site took off in an unruly fashion from all sides of the airfield. Keeping together, No. 253 Squadron's 'B' Flight climbed for height until they reached a few other Hurricanes flying at about 12,000 feet. The nervous tension was felt by all as the Hurricane pilots scanned the sky for German aircraft. The wait was soon over when a large formation of Dornier 17s and Messerschmitt 110s were sighted. Soaring straight into action, John turned his Hurricane after one of the bombers.

I got a Dornier in my sights but hadn't turned the gun sight on in my excitement; I did that, then pressed the gun button; but hadn't turned it on, so I did that. I then fired my guns and I think that I shot it down — one engine was on fire and it was not flying very well, but I could not follow it, as I was now engaged with 110s, so

I escaped by diving to the deck. We got back okay, except Jenkins, who crash-landed and came back by road. We had another patrol that afternoon but saw nothing and we only had five aircraft left for the next day.

The following morning the squadron took off and climbed steadily to a pre-determined height where they were supposed to rendezvous with some Fairey Battles and then escort them to Cambrai. Instead of meeting up with Battles, which were nowhere to be seen, they ran into some Messerschmitt 109s. In mere seconds the sky was full of aircraft turning in all directions as they fought for survival. In the confusion, John instantly became separated from his section over Lille. To evade the diving Me109s, John turned right into them and put his Hurricane into a dive. Pulling out of the dive at around 8,000 feet, he looked around to locate his position but soon found a lone Me109, which passed right underneath his aircraft at about 100 feet. Learning from his last combat experience, John made certain that his gun sight was on and his gun button ready to unleash the eight machine guns in his wings.

I fired from above and behind and watched all my deWilde ammunition going into the enemy. I was so excited that I thought the 109 was firing eight guns backwards straight into me. The enemy took no evasive action; it slowly nosed down and continued in a steep dive. I followed it down a little way but it was too steep a dive. I think the pilot was dead, as he did not jump out.

Combat Report Excerpt:
19 May 1940

At 10.30 I took off with three other pilots of B Flight to attack about 10 Me109s which had just shot down a Lysander. At 10.45 we had climbed to 10000 feet and I attacked one of the enemy from astern. The e/a dived and turned away, but I got in three bursts of about 6 seconds each. The enemy was then diving steeply and smoke was pouring from the engine. I pulled out of my dive and looked around for another enemy but saw nothing so returned to Lille to land and refuel.

When John landed back at the aerodrome, he was sad to discover that Flight Lieutenant Harry Anderson and Sergeant Gilbert MacKenzie had not returned. They had both been killed in action.

"When the ground party reached Boulogne, they were ordered to dump everything except firearms into the harbour, and there to this day remain my golfclubs."

Later that afternoon the remaining three squadron members took off for their final sortie of the day. Shortly after they had returned an order came through for them to fly back to Kenley, because the Germans had almost cut them off. With only three serviceable Hurricanes remaining, John took off with Clifton and Dawbarn and flew back across the English Channel. The Hurricanes left behind were broken up with axes, before the ground crew, led by Pilot Officer David Jenkins, set off for Boulogne in lorries.

When the ground party reached Boulogne, they were ordered to dump everything except firearms into the harbour, and there to this day remain my golf clubs, all my civilian clothes and uniform and great coat. We were reimbursed six days later with £25 to replace everything. I haven't forgotten or forgiven.

After three more sorties from Kenley, during which John claimed a Me109 as a 'probable', No. 253 Squadron lost its commanding officer; when Squadron Leader E. D. Elliot landed undamaged in France and was taken as a prisoner of war. The squadron was then sent to RAF Kirton in Lindsey, where it received a new commanding officer, new flight commanders and new pilots to replace those who had been lost, killed, or posted.

Aggression and Attrition

When the Battle of Britain was well under way, No. 253 Squadron had been re-equipped with improved Hurricanes that were fitted with Rotol props, armour plating and mirrors. John was particularly pleased with these new additions and felt more confident with their performance.

On the morning of 30 August 1940, nineteen aircraft of No. 253 Squadron took off from Kenley aerodrome and soon became involved in an aggressive fight with a swarm of Me110s.

I found myself head-on with one of these aircraft, and, having learnt my lesson in France, fired a short burst and dived steeply underneath him, pulling out at about 12,000 feet and re-oriented myself. Suddenly I saw a Heinkel 111 [of Kampfgeschwader 1] a short distance away and below me making for the coast; he had obviously been separated, with no other aircraft that I could see. I pounced on him from the port quarter and knocked both engines out. I followed him down and watched him make a good forced landing on the North Downs. Circling low down about 200 feet, I saw the crew of five leave their aircraft; one I saw covered in blood and lifted out by his comrades. Many years after the war, I discovered he died and another of the crew was wounded but lived. They were made POWs.

**Combat Report Excerpt:
30 August 1940**

Sighted enemy aircraft at 10-12,000 feet travelling S.E. of base. Delivered my attack from rear, firing all the ammunition I had left into the engines. The machine force landed in a field about 10 miles S.E. of base, somewhere near Edenbridge. Four of the crew climbed out, one hurt. The burst was about 8 seconds. The machine used no evasive tactics. Opened fire at 300 yards closing to 150 yards.

Although John had personally fared well against the Luftwaffe on this occasion, the squadron itself was badly hit. During this action three pilots were lost and two additional aircraft were damaged. Later in the day No. 253 suffered further loss when another pilot was lost and two Hurricanes downed. The battle was certainly taking its toll.

Still only 19 years old, John Greenwood continued to fight alongside his squadron comrades in the south of England. The constant patrols against the unrelenting enemy were arduous and stressful, yet the aerial conflict

JOHN GREENWOOD

raged on and more pilots were killed, wounded, and burned in blazing cockpits.

On 9 September 1940, No. 253's new commanding officer, Gerry Edge, led the squadron back into the fray against approximately forty Junkers 88s that were intending to bomb Hawkers at Kingston upon Thames. Flying in line abreast as the CO's number 2, John followed Edge into a head-on attack, but quickly realised he had no room to break off. John fired a short burst of ammunition at an oncoming Ju88 before ramming the stick forward to avoid collision. The Hurricane's engine cut out as the Ju88s passed closely overhead. Long after the war it was uncovered that German records claimed they had lost five aircraft of Kampfgeschwader 30 to the guns of No. 253 Squadron's Hurricanes on this encounter.

Because he had flown so many operational sorties with No. 253 Squadron from the outset, John Greenwood's experience became invaluable, and, as a consequence, at the end of his first period of operations, he was posted to No. 5 Flying Training School as an instructor. Although glad of the rest, John found instructing on Miles Masters incredibly dull. His spirits were soon lifted when in February 1941 he was sent to an Operational Training Unit to be an instructor.

After forming and instructing at No. 59 OTU, I volunteered for Merchant Ship Fighter Unit (MSFU) and, from May to November 1941, made four crossings of the North Atlantic in Empire Flame and the Novelist. It was so boring, taking about twenty-one days to cross the Atlantic with no sightings of either U-boats or Focke-Wulf Condors.

If it was more adventure that the pilot officer from Kingston was seeking, then it was certainly to follow, for the war was long and John Greenwood's service as a fighter pilot was anything but over. After a short spell at No. 55 OTU, John would rejoin an operational squadron, and take up duties in the Far East. ■

DAVID PRITCHARD

Left: Refuelling.

It is quite extraordinary, when reading about the exploits of Battle of Britain pilots, to learn how little experience many of them had on Spitfires or Hurricanes prior to their entry into the battle. The Royal Air Force desperately needed pilots following the losses of airmen in the Battle of France. With France overrun, the Germans set about preparing for the invasion of Britain. The Luftwaffe was tasked with achieving crucial air superiority. Britain was on the defensive. The RAF was on the defensive. RAF Fighter Command needed men to fly their weapons and it needed them quickly.

Becoming One of the Few

BILL GREEN

In the first part of his story, Battle of Britain pilot Bill Green describes the journey that took him from a boyhood flying aspiration to handling one of the Royal Air Force's front-line fighter aircraft, and then his experiences of the Battle of Britain. Bill entered the confrontation with the Luftwaffe with very few hours' experience of an operational aircraft and at one of the most crucial stages of the battle. It was, without doubt, a baptism of fire.

So You Want to Fly?
Bill Green was born on 23 April 1917 in Bristol, the son of a pre-1914 regular soldier, who was in France within days of the start of World War One, 'and was in the thick of the worst of it. In 1916 he developed sugar diabetes and was invalided out.' Bill's father died just before he was born. At the age of 14 Bill left school seeking work, and during the 1930s he set about developing a career in the

cardboard, printing, and packaging industry, during which he met his future wife, Bertha.

During this time Bill was encouraged to become involved in some kind of armed forces training. So he joined No. 501 Squadron Auxiliary Air Force, at Filton, as a fitter under training, in December 1936. Bill eventually sat an examination aspiring to go from an Aircraftman 2nd Class to an Aircraftman 1st Class, 'although if you achieved greater than 80 per cent you went straight to a Leading Aircraftman, at which point you finished your training and became part of a two-man crew under supervision'. Bill scored 84 per cent, 'Bang! I was an LAC.' In 1938, just after the September Munich 'Crisis', Bill's good friend, a rigger, informed him that he was leaving to become a pilot with the Royal Air Force Volunteer Reserve. 'I was nearly sick with envy. He had left school at 18 and had a good education whereas I had left at 14. They wouldn't

Below: Bill Green and Bertha at Lyme Regis in 1937.

BILL GREEN

BILL GREEN'S HURRICANE ILLUSTRATION BY PETE WEST

even have looked at me.' Bill wrote to the commanding officer of No. 501 Squadron and asked for permission to leave, to join the Volunteer Reserve to become a pilot. The CO, Squadron Leader Clube, sent for Bill.

'So Green you want to fly do you?'

'Yes sir.'

'Why?'

'Well I just want to fly.'

'Hmm. Wouldn't you rather stay with the squadron and fly.'

'Yes, but that's only for commissioned people.'

'Well I am getting an establishment for six NCO pilots and you could become a sergeant pilot. Wouldn't you rather be one of those?'

Well it was like asking the cat if he would like to be thrown in a barrel of cream. So I remustered from LAC fitter to LAC pilot u/t (under training), January 1939. There was a pilot officer instructor, who was also the adjutant, and Clube the CO, who were regulars. All the rest were acting pilot officers or pilot officers auxiliary air force. I was always at the end of the queue for time to fly, and got less flying in than the rest of them. With that, the English weather, and the limited time I was able to be there, I had done ten hours dual by the time war started and hadn't gone solo. We were mobilised on 14 August 1939, and in October I was sent away to No. 5 Elementary Flying Training School at RAF Hanworth.

Bill carried out his first solo flight in October 1939 in a Miles Magister. 'That was beyond description. The joy. I remember taking off and thinking I'm in the air, I'm in the air, on my own. I wrote to Bertha that night and expressed my joy.'

Bill built up experience at EFTS and was then posted to No. 3 Flying Training School at South Cerney on Hawker Harts. Through March 1940 Bill accumulated flying hours.

Bertha and I had been courting for a number of years and we planned to be married. I was at South Cerney in May 1940 when the Battle of France was collapsing and all leave was cancelled. We had already had our bands called to be married in Bristol, but that was gone because I couldn't get leave. So Bertha got on the bus and came up to Cirencester. I was on night flying and had the day off on 3 June for sleeping, but instead of sleeping we were

intending to get married. Anyway at the last moment the CO relented and gave me a 48-hour pass. We were married on 3 June 1940 in Cirencester.

Midway through July 1940 Bill returned to No. 501 Squadron, then at RAF Middle Wallop, under the command of a new CO, Squadron Leader Harry Hogan.

A wonderful man. I presented myself and he asked me to tell him about who I was. He said 'What have you flown?' So I told him. He said, 'Have you flown anything with radio?'

'No.'

'Retractable undercarriage, flaps, oxygen, enclosed cockpit?'

'No, no, no, no.'

'Have you fired any guns?'

'No.'

'You're no earthly good to me. I'm going to send you off to an operational training unit; they are starting one at Aston Down, near Bristol. You go home and you'll get a telegram sending you there.'

So I hitchhiked home that day and when I got home there was a telegram telling me to report to Uxbridge. I thought this was odd. I knew Uxbridge to be a recruiting air station. So I went to a telephone box.

Frustration

Bill called RAF Uxbridge and told them he had a telegram and got the reply, 'Oh, you want the BBC.'

I put the phone down, dialled again, got another voice, and told him the same tale. He said, 'Oh, you want the BBC.' I put the phone down again and said to Bertha, 'Oh to hell with it. I'm not going back today'. I went the next day up to Uxbridge, checked into the guardroom and was told I wanted the PDC, Personnel Despatch Centre. So down I go and there was this snotty little acting pilot officer there and he said, 'Oh, oh, who are you?' I told him. 'Well what were you doing before you were flying, were you a tradesman?' I said yes I was a fitter. 'You are for Takoradi on the Gold Coast, go down to stores and get your overseas kit.' I was in Alice in Wonderland. One minute I was going to OTU, next minute I'm in Uxbridge, and now I'm going to Takoradi. I got to the stores and the corporal piled up the shorts and the shirts. He said, 'Sign here sergeant.'

'I'm not going to sign that.'

'Why not. Don't you want to go to Takoradi?'

'No I don't.'

'Oh it's wonderful there. You either enjoy boisterous health there, in which case you'll die within six weeks of getting home, or you'll die within six weeks of getting there.'

I walked out and went back to this chap and said, 'Can I please phone my adjutant?'

'Why?'

'I don't think I'm supposed to be going to Takoradi. I'm supposed to be going to an OTU.'

'What's that?'

'An Operational Training Unit.'

'I'll phone him,' he said. Apparently I wasn't capable of using a telephone. He came back and said, 'You're quite right, quite right. Go down to the football stadium.'

Jargon and Diction

Bill did indeed go to the football stadium, only to find it empty.

There was one stand so I went there. I could hear voices and followed these to a room. There were a number of other people, mostly commissioned, if not all. There was a big table with the south-west of England drawn on it.

There was a chappy in charge of this, connected with the BBC. He said, 'The air is full of chatter; with so many aeroplanes we can't afford that. You are going to learn jargon, which the Royal Air Force are going to introduce and I will also help you with your diction. We are going to do this by means of learning about how the plotting works and how radar works, and what you will be subjected to when you are back in your squadron.'

So we had an exercise where you were either the controller or one of the plotter shovers or you were the radar. There was a hole in the roof, with a ladder, and if you were the radar man you were up there. The airfield had been marked out in squares, with letters or numbers and at one end of the airfield there were three Wall's ice cream bicycles, with TR9 radio sets in a helmet. And at the other end was one bicycle with no radio. When the controller downstairs phoned up to the bloke on the roof, and said 'Scramble', he would fire a red from a Verey pistol. The 'bomber' bloke was instructed, when he saw the red Verey, to start cycling towards the other end, but not in a straight line, changing course. And every time he changed course the chap on the roof would telephone down '200 bandits, square 1', or whatever, and the plotter would react. At the same time the Controller would scramble the fighter leader who was sitting on the first of the three ice cream bicycles at the far end. He

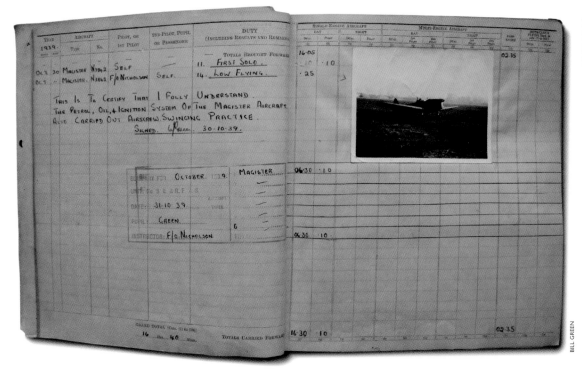

Left: Bill Green's logbook, recording his first solo flight on 30 October 1939.

would then give them courses and you would see them take this course, or that course, to intercept the bomber. It was an exercise in interception, how the radar worked, and how the plotting worked.

At the end of this, the professor from the BBC said, 'I'm going to put on a record and I want you to tell me what you hear.' It sounded like speeded-up chipmunks. 'Does anyone know what it is?' he asked. We all laughed, there was no way. So he played it again and asked us again. Well someone said they thought it was such and such, but we were guessing. So he said, 'Now I'm going to tell you what it says and then I'll play it again. It's simply saying "Mary, Mary quite contrary, how does your garden grow".' He played it again and it was all crystal clear. Unbelievably. 'That is because', he said, 'you were trying to unscramble the message and you were imagining it might be this or that or the other. When you had a disciplined expectation you heard it clearly. To convince the brass of the Royal Air Force with this I'll tell you what happened. We assembled them and I picked

the whole point. Then he would play through our recorded exchange and correct the diction. It was a wonderfully simplistic idea of introducing me to what it was all about.

'Just Take it Off'

Three days later Bill returned to RAF Middle Wallop to find the squadron had moved to RAF Gravesend.

I found my way there and Squadron Leader Hogan said, 'Now what's been happening to you Green?' I told him. 'Well we'll not bother with an OTU. You get yourself to Biggin Hill and they have a Master there and you'll learn how to fly.'

On 3 August 1940 Bill and Pilot Officer Keith Aldridge flew to RAF Biggin Hill and reported into the training flight.

A Flying Officer Flinders was in charge. He said, 'Our Master is u/s, you had better get on over to Hornchurch.

Right: Bill Green's logbook, recording his first flight in a Hurricane on 8 August 1940.

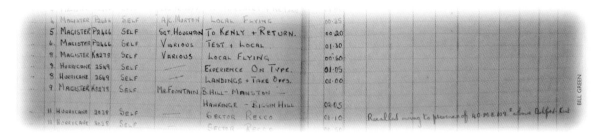

Right: Bill Green's logbook, recording his first flight in a Hurricane on 8 August 1940.

up the telephone. They were all listening. And the operator at the other end said, 'Number please.'

'The gentlemen of Wembley are a motley assembly.'

'I'm sorry sir. I didn't get your number.'

'The gentlemen of Wembley are a motley assembly.'

'I'm sorry sir I didn't get your Wembley number.'

'I am not saying a number I am saying the gentlemen of Wembley are a motley assembly.'

The professor had then got a mouthful from her, as she didn't have time to waste 'talking to idiots'. He said to the brass that was because she was expecting to hear a number and she didn't understand the Wembley bit. Then she was still expecting a number and said she didn't understand the Wembley number.

'When I told her', he said, 'that I wasn't saying that I got the answer I should have had first of all if she hadn't been trying to unscramble my message.' That was

They've got one over there.' So we did. He had two circuits, dual and one solo, in the Master, and I clambered into this strange new beast and flew one dual circuit with the instructor. He said, 'Oh you're OK, you're fine. Go and get back to Biggin. No time for you to go solo tonight.'

Over the next few days Bill flew the odd solo in a Magister, and then, on 8 August 1940, it was time to get to grips with an operational aircraft, the Hawker Hurricane.

Flinders said to me, 'Now then Green. What were you before you were a pilot?' I must have smelt of being a fitter. I said, 'Well, I was a fitter.' He said, 'What did you have?' I said, 'We had just got our first Hurricane.' And he said, 'Well you know all about it then. Look there's one over there. Go and sit in it and when you feel happy about it just take it off.' I said, 'Well hang on. I've never flown anything like this really. What speed does it lift off at and what speed does it come in at and what speed do you have for a loop and a roll and so on and so forth.' So he rattled these off and I went and sat in this Hurricane. After a bit I thought well I had better get on with it I suppose. So I signalled the crew and they started it up and away I went. I frightened myself to death! I went up to about 20,000 feet. Here I was in this enclosed cockpit with a mask on, with oxygen on, radio messages going on all the time about activity that was going on in the air. I added about 50 per cent to the speeds he had given me, I suppose for safety, and did this loop, pulled my stick back like I would have done in the Hart and blacked out with the 'g'. When I came round, the instruments were all going round the cockpit because they were gyro operated. Nobody had said to me you had to lock them before you did any aerobatics. I was upside down, inverted, hanging in my straps. I put my stick over to roll out of it and went into a spin. The buzz was that Hurricanes and Spitfires wouldn't come out of a spin. Well, I thought, I've got to try anyway. So I did my correcting action, which was full opposite rudder and stick forward to unshield the elevator, and soon as it came out of the spin you centralised and then eased it out of the ensuing dive. Well I did the correcting action and sure enough it came out of the spin. I must have been so full of the joy of being normal, as it were, that I didn't centralise, and I immediately went into a spin the other way. So when I finally got out of it and centralised, I was quite lowish anyway, there was no horizon, I was below the horizon, because of the haze, and the instruments were going all round the cockpit. It was quite nauseating really. Anyway, I found my way back to Biggin and realised too late to make any difference that I was overshooting. I thought I would get it down all right; I'm nothing if not overconfident. I landed it halfway up the runway, ran out of runway, where all the Hurricanes were parked, and zigzagged my way, missing them, and finished up about a yard from the hedge at the end of the airfield. I sat there with the aeroplane intact, and I was intact, and I tell you it was some sense of relief to be down in one piece. I felt totally relieved and a little proud that I had managed it. Whereupon Squadron Leader Worrall, the CO of 32 Squadron, jumped up on to the mainplane and gave me one hell of a strip. I can't begin to tell you all the language he used or what he said, apart from 'Report to my office.' So I went in, he had calmed

down a bit by then, and he said, 'What were you doing?' So I told him it was my first flight and what had happened. 'Well we'll forget the fortnight confined to camp,' he said. 'But don't ever doing anything like that again. You could have written off half a dozen aeroplanes, which we valuably need, and yourself. Don't ever do that again.' And that was my first flight in a Hurricane.

Over the course of the next week or so most of Bill's flights involved delivering aircraft to other RAF stations.

Then on 19 August I delivered a Hurricane to Gravesend and ran slap bang into Hogan. He said, 'How you getting on?' I replied that I had done about six or seven hours. 'Oh they're much too slow training you over there. You had better get back here. We'll train you much more quickly.' I asked when he wanted me back. 'Tonight!'

Entering the Battle
Bill returned in a Magister and was given a bed alongside 'Ginger' Lacey, who had seen considerable action during the Battle of France, and had already claimed enemy aircraft during the Battle of Britain. 'I went off with him, had a cup of cocoa and a cheese sandwich and then got my head down.'

At 3 a.m., in the dark, there was a light flashing in my face. I said, 'No not me. I've just arrived. I'm Green.' 'I know,' he said, 'you're Green 3.' So I found myself walking down to the aeroplane just before dawn with Ginger Lacey.

'What's all this about? What's this Green 3, Ginger?' I asked.

'We're the arse-end Charlie flight. When we get some height, we weave about at the back of the other nine to make sure that we're not bounced. When you see me do a turn to the right, you do a turn to the left. Don't go too far or you'll lose the squadron.'

Once in the air Bill 'did the gentlest and shortest turn of all time', but when he had turned back 'they'd all gone. When they're doing 300 one way and you're doing 300 another way, it doesn't take long to lose sight of them. I found my way down to Hawkinge.'

From 19 to 23 August 1940 there was a general lull in the battle over Britain, cloudy weather providing both sides with an opportunity to regroup, although Bill Green

did confront the enemy, as recorded in his logbook.

Then, on 24 August 1940, the weather cleared and the Luftwaffe once more attacked in force. For the Germans to launch an invasion successfully, the Royal Air Force simply had to be destroyed. The target was the entire British air organisation, the aircraft industry, the air defence system, the fighter aircraft and pilots, and the airfields. Flying in defence of one of those airfields was Bill Green.

We were scrambled and vectored towards Manston. There were some Ju88s and we were hastening towards them and suddenly there was an explosion. The aeroplane was

occasional patrol but without encountering the enemy. Then on 28 August Bill was 'attacked by a Hurricane'.

Later that day Bill received the welcome news that he was being rested for a short time.

The tannoy went telling us our flight was released for 24 hours. Percy Morfill — a pre-war airman, wonderful man, ultra experienced — and I had agreed that, if ever we got a day release, we would nobble the Magister, and I would drop him at White Waltham and then go on to Bristol. I would then pick him up again the next day in time to be at Gravesend for midday and in time for

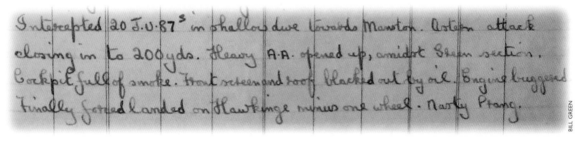

jolted and the front windscreen was black with oil. The aeroplane coughed and spluttered, and then picked up again. I could see little or nothing through this black film on the windscreen, so I was peering out of the sides. I got it back to Hawkinge and landed it, but it went up on its nose. I finished up vertical to the ground but I was OK, not injured.*

Shot Down

Over the course of the next few days Bill regularly flew between Gravesend and Hawkinge, carrying out the

readiness. My wife had knitted me a pair of socks; she was with her mother in Bristol at that time. She saw me off at Whitchurch airfield. I wore these socks and I picked up Morfill and we went back.

In the afternoon, we were at readiness. I was writing to Bertha from the dispersal tent saying how much I had enjoyed my time with her at home and not to worry because I knew everything was going to be fine and we weren't going to be flying that day anyway because the cloud was down to about 300 feet, solid.

At six o'clock, after I had written the letter, we were

scrambled and went up through 12,000 feet of cloud, independently, and then reassembled over the tops of the cloud. We had this message, 'Go to Red Queen', the codename for Deal, then 'Angels 20'.

We went to Deal at 20,000 feet and were ordered to orbit; we split up, orbiting independently. I was rubbernecking through 360 degrees above, all the time; the danger always came from above. Suddenly there was a crash of glass and a hole appeared in my windscreen bigger than a tennis ball. I could hear the glass tingling. It was an inch and a quarter thick, supposedly bullet proof. Simultaneously I had liquid spraying all over me. The control column was like a piece of wood in my hand. I had no control. I knew I had to get out. I pulled the pin of the Sutton harness, which strapped me into the aeroplane, and I started to get to my feet and then 'fwoopp' — I was out. I thought at the time that the aeroplane had exploded and I had been blown out. I found myself out of the aeroplane and rolling. I thought 'By God, I'll never find the rip cord.' I remember on the first roll hearing my flying boots go, 'psst, psst'. My legs would have been spread-eagled and bear in mind the boots were strapped up to the knee; but notwithstanding, the violence of my rolling kicked them off. I thought I would never find the rip cord but eventually I did. 'Great,' I thought, it was all over. I yanked it, still rolling.

You sat on your parachute, and a drogue parachute, a small one, had springs inside it compressed and trapped in the outer layer of the canvas parachute pack by the end of the rip cord — a needle that went through three holes. When you pulled the pin, it decompressed, and the air hit it and dragged the main parachute out of its folded state under your bottom. Something white came out and I watched it. I thought it was going round, but it was me going round. It was going away from me as I was descending. Almost at the same time the main canopy must have fallen from its pack, and it came up through my legs, and wrapped itself around me. I couldn't see anything, wrapped in this folded parachute. I tried to push it back, still rolling, forlornly of course. I know I had been falling for a long, long time and I know I must have been thinking of my end. I remember so clearly thinking that I wonder if Bertha will wonder if I wondered, as I fell, what my end was going to be like. She will realise, as I was realising, that it will be this and then black, everything will go black and that will be it. This and then nothing.

I was continuing to struggle. Either the parachute had to become inflated and kick me back, or I had to stop rolling this way and roll the other way. All of a sudden, amid the confusion and thoughts, there was a jolt and immediately a second jolt. I thought the whole lot might be going, so I grabbed the straps. There was quietude beyond any noise you can describe. Suddenly nothing. I thought, 'God. I'm alive.' I looked to my left and the trees were above me. I looked to the right and the pylon electricity cables were level with me. The only thing I had learned was that you had to relax your legs when you hit the ground. I did and bang I was on the ground.

I sat on this sloping field with thistles and cowpats all over the place, in my brand new socks. I sat there thinking, have I got to walk through all this in my stockinged feet. I don't know why I thought that; perhaps I was semi-stunned. At that moment two blokes came running down the field, one of whom had a shot gun. When they got near, I heard one of them say, 'Oh, he's

Below: Bill Green's logbook entry for 29 August 1940.

Scramble at 18.00 hrs to 20,000' above Deal. Squadron attacked while orbitting, by 200 plus 109's. Hit from astern by aircraft in the sun. First burst; large hole in bulletproof windscreen, instruments shattered with terrible demoralising crash. Petrol and glycol leaking like a drain. Little or no control. Aircraft exploded: Blown out: Boots flicked off. Pulled chord. Pilot chute detached. Wrapped in chute, while rolling and struggling violently. Parachute opens finally at 0–300'. Wounded in legs by cannon splinters. Lucky Break

-30   How Green was my valley   Dec 1943

British.' I went to get up but couldn't. Then I realised I had been hit in the knee. They helped me back to the farmhouse and gave me a cup of tea.

Bill was taken back to Hawkinge, and to sick quarters, where he was met by a Flying Officer Samuels, 'with a long needle'. 'It was like a knitting needle, steel. There was a hole in my knee about as big as my little finger, as though a pencil had been cleanly pushed in. He started probing around in there and I fainted.'

Bill Green's Battle of Britain was over, although he would be returning to operational duties, after which he did some instructing and then flew Hawker Typhoons and Tempests supporting the advance through Europe, following the 1944 Allied Normandy landings. The second part of Bill Green's story will be appearing in a future volume of Fighting High —World War Two — Air Battle Europe. ∎

Below:
Bill Green, 2009.

A Hero's
Tragedy

The date 15 September 1940 is regarded as the decisive day of the Battle of Britain. The Luftwaffe threw itself into an all-out attack on London, and RAF Fighter Command pilots took to the skies to oppose the aggressors in force. By the end of the day news had spread across England that an incredible 185 enemy aircraft had been shot down. This proved to be a considerable overstatement, as history would eventually record a loss rate at a third of that originally claimed. Nevertheless, at the time it proved to be a massive boost to morale for both the public and the Royal Air Force. The German Air Force had believed Fighter Command was on the edge of defeat, but pilots like No. 19 Squadron's Flying Officer Leonard Haines had forced them to think again.

IWM CH 1373

LEONARD A. HAINES' SPITFIRE MK1A ILLUSTRATION BY PETE WEST

No. 19 Squadron's Leonard Haines's first successes came while he was supporting the evacuation of Allied troops from Dunkirk at the beginning of June 1940, when he claimed a Messerschmitt 109 and a Heinkel 111 probable.

He would go on to become an 'Ace' of the Battle of Britain, flying with No. 19 Squadron, and he also earned a Distinguished Flying Cross. Leonard's combat reports demonstrate his combat abilities.

Opposite page:
Flying Officer Leonard A. Haines of No. 19 Squadron RAF sits by the cockpit of his Supermarine Spitfire Mark IA at Fowlmere, Cambridgeshire.

```
DATE:                          1.6.40
FLIGHT, SQUADRON:              Sqdn: 19
NUMBER OF ENEMY AIRCRAFT:      15-20
TYPE OF ENEMY AIRCRAFT:        Me109, Me110 (Jaguars)
TIME ATTACK WAS DELIVERED:     0540
PLACE ATTACK WAS DELIVERED:    2 miles N.E. Dunkirk
HEIGHT OF ENEMY:               4000 feet
ENEMY CASUALTIES:              1 Me109 certain
```

I was flying with 19 Squadron on patrol over the Dunkirk area. On sighting the enemy I delivered a deflection attack upon an E/A to within 20 yards. The enemy aircraft dived vertically into the ground with glycol streaming from it.
No. of rounds fired - 200

```
DATE:                          1.6.40
FLIGHT, SQUADRON:              Sqdn: 19
NUMBER OF ENEMY AIRCRAFT:      15-20
TYPE OF ENEMY AIRCRAFT:        He.111, Do. 215
TIME ATTACK WAS DELIVERED:     0955
PLACE ATTACK WAS DELIVERED:    Over Dunkirk
HEIGHT OF ENEMY:               3000 feet
ENEMY CASUALTIES:              1 He. 111 probable
```

Climbing attack from port quarter opening fire at 200 yards range port engine burst into flames almost directly and I followed through until attack closing to within 50 yards meeting with no fire whatsoever and finishing up dead astern. The e/a continued gliding steeply towards the sea with engine blazing fiercely.

Flying from RAF Duxford and the nearby airfield at Fowlmere, No. 19 Squadron, as part of No. 12 Group, saw considerable action during the Battle of Britain. Leonard Haines was in the thick of the action as the battle escalated through the end of August and into September 1940. The Luftwaffe frantically sought to neutralise their opposing air force. Leonard Haines and his Fighter Command colleagues were desperate not to relinquish command of the skies.

```
DATE:                          19.8.40
FLIGHT, SQUADRON:              Green Section. Flight: B. Sqdn: 19
NUMBER OF ENEMY AIRCRAFT:      1
TYPE OF ENEMY AIRCRAFT:        Me.110
TIME ATTACK WAS DELIVERED:     1845
PLACE ATTACK WAS DELIVERED:    8 miles East of Aldeburgh
HEIGHT OF ENEMY:               4000 feet
ENEMY CASUALTIES:              1 certain (shared)
```

I was leading Green Section and was given a vector sending me to Aldeburgh when Green 3 reported that there was an enemy aircraft ahead of us approx 1000 feet higher. I recognised the enemy aircraft as being an Me. 110 and ordered line astern. The enemy aircraft headed for a cloud and was attacked by Green 2 and followed through cloud by Green 3 - Green 1 going above cloud and meeting enemy aircraft the other side. The enemy aircraft was being attacked by a machine-gun Spitfire just before I attacked but no apparent damage was being done. I made an attack from dead astern of enemy fire at 350 yards and closing to 150 yards by which time my cannons had stopped firing.

I noticed a piece of main plane shot away and the port engine stopped dead. I then saw another machine - confirmed to be Green 3 attacking and after he had broken away the enemy aircraft slowly burst into flames and crashed into the sea. I noticed four people bale out, apparently all from enemy aircraft which rather suggests that enemy aircraft was an Me. Jaguar. Tracer fire was coming from both upper and lower rear guns. There was a large amount of cumulus cloud at 5000 feet and approx 3/10 at 2000 feet and the sun was obscured. I had taken off from G.1 at 1809 hours and landed at G.1 1925 hours.

DATE:	3.9.40
FLIGHT, SQUADRON:	Green Section. Flight: B. Sqdn: 19
NUMBER OF ENEMY AIRCRAFT:	50 Bombers 100 Me.110
TYPE OF ENEMY AIRCRAFT:	Only Me.110 recognised
TIME ATTACK WAS DELIVERED:	Approx 1030
PLACE ATTACK WAS DELIVERED:	Between Colchester and Thames Estuary.
HEIGHT OF ENEMY:	20,000 feet
ENEMY CASUALTIES:	1 Me 110 certain

I was on patrol with 19 Squadron leading Green Section at a height of 20,000 over base when we sighted black smoke coming from the direction of North Weald. On investigation we observed approx 50 Bombers in tight formation with numerous Me.110's stepped up behind them as escort and went into attack the Me.110's. I noticed one Me.110 by itself in front and above the bombers but on attacking it, it dived towards the enemy bombers so I broke off the attack. I then noticed 2 Me.110 on my right and just below so I immediately closed into a range of 250 yards and opened fire. The other Me.110 dived away and I pressed home my attack. The enemy aircraft was camouflaged greyish above with black crosses on main planes and egg shell blue underneath. After a burst of approx 5 seconds during which the enemy aircraft employed various tactics, steep turns climbing and diving. I noticed some smoke coming from the port engine and the enemy aircraft dived vertically towards Thames. I followed it down and just when I thought it was going straight in it flattened out and headed towards Whitstable at about 50 feet off the water. Accordingly I followed it occasionally closed in to approx 100 yards whenever he was in a favourable position as in a climb. Two lines of tracer fire coming from rear turret were passing beneath me at commencement of attack.

When nearing Whitstable the enemy aircraft turned back and headed towards mouth of Thames flying straight and level and with smoke coming from port engine. I let it have the rest of my ammunition from 100 yards dead astern and I noticed a piece of fabric fly off and the enemy aircraft plunged into the sea.

Took off G.1. 1015 hours, landed G.1. 1125 hours.

DATE:	5.9.40
FLIGHT, SQUADRON:	Flight: 'B' Green Section Sqdn: 19
NUMBER OF ENEMY AIRCRAFT:	Approx 40 Me110 & numerous Me109
TYPE OF ENEMY AIRCRAFT:	Me110, Me109 and bombers
TIME ATTACK WAS DELIVERED:	Approx 10.10
PLACE ATTACK WAS DELIVERED:	Began near Chatham ended at Ashford
HEIGHT OF ENEMY:	16,000 feet
ENEMY CASUALTIES:	1 Me109 destroyed

General Report. Whilst leading Green section on a patrol over Chatham numerous E/A were sighted at approx 10.05 hrs. Enemy formation consisted of unidentified bombers, Me110s and Me109 and were heading south-west. Line astern was ordered and whilst following Blue leader into the enemy formation I was attacked by two Me109. I did a steep turn and as they dived passed me I opened up my engine and chased the second one. I waited until I was at 200 yards range and opened fire. After a five second burst the E/A's engine began issuing puffs of smoke and the pilot began hedge hopping. I kept in range and let him have the rest of my ammunition when I noticed a burst of flame from the engine and it issued a continuous stream of black smoke. He was then over the fields and approaching Ashford. On reaching more or less the centre of the town he climbed his aircraft to 800 feet and baled out. The E/A crashed in flames in the garden of a house and the pilot landed safely in a field.

The E/A was camouflaged in the normal way and the pilot tried various evasive tactics in an endeavour to shake me off his tail.

There was no cloud in area of combat and the sun was mostly behind me.

I had taken off from G1 at 0947 hours and landed at 1100 hours.

DATE:	11/9/40
FLIGHT, SQUADRON:	Flight: 'B' Sqdn: 19
NUMBER OF ENEMY AIRCRAFT:	
TYPE OF ENEMY AIRCRAFT:	He111, Me110, Me109
TIME ATTACK WAS DELIVERED:	16.30 hours
PLACE ATTACK WAS DELIVERED:	Gravesend
HEIGHT OF ENEMY:	20,000 feet
ENEMY CASUALTIES:	1 Me110 certain

General Report. Whilst leading Green Section on a patrol over Gravesend we encountered large forces of E/A consisting of He.111 Me.110 and Me.109. The C.O. attacked a bunch of He.111 and I climbed slightly, to engage a force of some 40 Me.110's which were a little higher and to the East. The E/A went into a defensive circle when I attacked and I only managed to get in a 1 second burst at the nearest one which was about 300 yards away. I broke off the attack and waited until I noticed one which was a little lower than

the rest. I closed to 200 yards and opened fire. The E/A's starboard engine burst into flames and it broke formation, I followed it and gave it a long burst when the port engine caught fire and lots of pieces came away from the fuselage and port mainplane. I had observed no rear fire but was continually having to evade attacks by Me.109 - which were painted yellow from spinner to cockpit - which dived on me from above.

After the combat I noticed several bullet holes in both mainplanes, but as the aircraft appeared quite normal in flight, I climbed and endeavoured to engage some more Me110s. E/A went into a defensive circle on sighting me and when I tried to get above them they climbed also. I kept in their vicinity and they gradually climbed from 15,000 ft to 20,000 ft, and made towards the Coast. I had to leave them over Beachy Head not having been able to engage one, unfortunately.

My aircraft crashed on landing as both tyres had been punctured by bullets. I had taken off from G.1 and crash landed at G1.

BATTLE OF BRITAIN DAY · 15 SEPTEMBER 1940

Late on the morning of 15 September 1940 British radar picked up a considerable enemy attack developing, and Fighter Command's squadrons prepared to meet the assault. No. 11 Group first met the attackers over Kent and the south of London, before No. 12 Group's Duxford Wing, including No. 19 Squadron Spitfires, tangled with the enemy formations over London itself.

The No. 19 Squadron Operations Record Book recorded that at 1130 hours the squadron had taken off to patrol with the Wing and 'Waded straight into party over London area. Approx 250–300 E/A., all types.' Numerous pilots made claims, including Flying Officer Leonard Haines.

```
DATE:                        15/9/40
FLIGHT, SQUADRON:            Flight: 'B' Sqdn: 19
NUMBER OF ENEMY AIRCRAFT:    Unknown
TYPE OF ENEMY AIRCRAFT:      Do215s & Me109 only recognised.
TIME ATTACK WAS DELIVERED:   Approx 1250 hours
PLACE ATTACK WAS DELIVERED:  West of & near Biggin Hill
HEIGHT OF ENEMY:             20,000 feet
ENEMY CASUALTIES:            1 Me109 certain
```

```
General Report. Whilst leading Green Section on a patrol, South of London I noticed
A.A. fire just West of London and on investigating I noticed a force of some forty E/A
which I could not identify. I put my Section into line astern and made toward A.A.
fire, when two Me109s appeared to my right. I accordingly turned and attacked them. I
gave one a burst (deflection from above) and it half rolled and dived vertically to
12,000 ft. where it straightened out. I had dived after it and as soon as it finished
its dive I re-commenced my attack. I was going faster than the E/A and I continued
firing until I had to pull away to the right to avoid collision. The E/A half rolled
and dived vertically with black smoke coming from underneath the pilot's seat it
seemed. I followed it down until it entered cloud at about 6,000 ft. and had to
recover from the dive as E/A was then going at approx. 480 m.p.h. I then made my way
through the cloud at a reasonable speed and found the wreckage of E/A burning
furiously. It was painted yellow from spinner to cockpit.
I climbed up through cloud and narrowly missed colliding with a Ju.88 which was
on fire and being attacked by numerous Hurricanes. Unfortunately I could not make
further contact with the enemy and returned to base.
     I had taken off from G.1 at 11.30 hours and landed at 13.50 hours.
```

Following a few hours' respite, Fighter Command was once more warned by radar that another vast armada of Luftwaffe bombers and fighters was approaching, heading for London. Once more the pilots of the Royal Air Force met their opponent. Once more the Duxford Wing's pilots tore into the enemy. The No. 19 Squadron ORB recorded 'another party along with Wing . . . when we arrived the formation had already been broken up by 11 Group'. Again numerous claims were made, and once more Leonard Haines was in the midst of the fighting.

```
DATE:                        15/9/40
FLIGHT, SQUADRON:            Flight: 'B' Sqdn: 19
NUMBER OF ENEMY AIRCRAFT:    200
TYPE OF ENEMY AIRCRAFT:      Do17, He111, Me110, Me109
TIME ATTACK WAS DELIVERED:   Me109 - 1440 approx. Me110 - 1450 approx
PLACE ATTACK WAS DELIVERED:  Me109 over Thames Estuary
                             Me110 over Beachy Head
HEIGHT OF ENEMY:             28,000ft. Me109. 17,000ft. Me110
ENEMY CASUALTIES:            1 Me109 cert. 1 Me110 cert.
```

General Report. I was leading Green section on a patrol when Blue Leader sighted and attacked six Do17. Just before following him I noticed five Me109 above and to my right so I accordingly climbed to attack. On reaching the same height the E/A formed a defensive circle but I managed to fire a burst at one which did the usual half roll and dived. I followed him down, and at approx 15000' he flattened out so I closed in and let him have a 5 sec. burst from 300-50 yards range. He burst into flames and disappeared into the cloud in a vertical dive.

I then climbed to approx 25,000' and patrolled the coast near Beachy Head. After waiting some five minutes I noticed a large force of enemy bombers being attacked by Hurricanes. They were escorted by numerous Me110s which circled when they noticed me. After waiting some time I noticed two slightly behind the others so I closed into 250 yards range with one and fired a burst of approx. 5 secs. when his starboard engine burst into flames and he dived steeply.

As I was meeting return fire I closed to approx 150 yards and let E/A have the rest of my ammunition.

At the end of my attack I noticed the rear gun draped along the fuselage.

E/A went through the clouds with bits coming off the starboard wing. I followed him and E/A just reached the French coast and crashed in flames on the beach. I darted back into clouds and returned home.

I had left G.1. at 1415 hrs and landed G.1. at 1540 hrs.

The claims of 15 September 1940 took Leonard Haines to seven enemy aircraft destroyed, one probable and one shared. But he would go on to make further claims in 1940, adding one further aircraft destroyed, three more shared and another probable. In the meantime, his abilities and bravery were recognised with the award of a Distinguished Flying Cross on 8 October 1940.

Left: A Supermarine Spitfire Mark 1A of No 19 Squadron, Royal Air Force, being rearmed between sorties at Fowlmere, Cambridgeshire.

DATE: 18/9/40
FLIGHT, SQUADRON: Flight: 'B' Sqdn: 19
NUMBER OF ENEMY AIRCRAFT: 22 approx
TYPE OF ENEMY AIRCRAFT: Ju.88 He.111 Me.109
TIME ATTACK WAS DELIVERED: 1725
PLACE ATTACK WAS DELIVERED: Over Thames Estuary
HEIGHT OF ENEMY: 15,000ft.
ENEMY CASUALTIES: 1 Ju.88 (shared with Blue 2)
                                    1 Me109 probable

General Report. Whilst leading Green section on a patrol near London approximately 20 E/A were observed heading S.E. at 5,000 ft. Over Thames Estuary. We accordingly attacked and after firing a burst of 4 secs at a Ju.88 the starboard engine began smoking. This E/A was subsequently attacked by Blue 2 and set on fire. When I climbed for another attack I was engaged by 2 Me109's which I chased and attacked. I was surprised to observe fire coming from a single m.g. mounted laterally and seemingly just under or behind the pilot's seat, from one of them. I concentrated on this one and let him have a long burst at 200-50 yds. then he half rolled and dived vertically with black smoke pouring from his engine. Whether this was due to my fire or whether it was because he had opened up fully I cannot say. I watched him dive into the clouds at high speed and began searching for the other E/A which I failed to find unfortunately so I returned to base. I had taken off from G.1 at 1625 and landed at 1800 hours.

DATE: 5/11/40
FLIGHT, SQUADRON: Flight: 'B' Sqdn: 19
NUMBER OF ENEMY AIRCRAFT: 25 approximately
TYPE OF ENEMY AIRCRAFT: Me109's and He. 113
TIME ATTACK WAS DELIVERED: 16.15 - 1630 hours
PLACE ATTACK WAS DELIVERED: Thames Estuary to Birchington
HEIGHT OF ENEMY: 26,500ft.
ENEMY CASUALTIES: One Me109 destroyed (shared)

General Report. Whilst leading 'B' Flight on a Wing patrol over Thames estuary, we encountered a number of Me.109's flying approximately 2,000 feet above us. We climbed to attack and E/A kept diving out of the sun past me but every time I managed to get within range of one my windscreen would ice up and I couldn't see a thing. I decided to attack one Me.109 which passed approximately 400 yds. in front of me. At 200 yds. I gave him a short burst and he dived to 2,000 feet. At the end of his dive I let him have a long burst at 200-100 yds. range when I noticed a small stream of black coming from underneath the engine and he slowed up considerably. As I had no more ammunition I formatted on his right side and let a Hurricane, piloted by P/O W.L. McKnight, give E/A a long burst at about 150 yds. range when bits came off starboard wing, engine began issuing a larger stream of black smoke and pilot baled out, landing in a tree at Birchington, Kent.

DATE: 15/11/40
FLIGHT, SQUADRON: Flight: 'B' Sqdn: 19
NUMBER OF ENEMY AIRCRAFT: One
TYPE OF ENEMY AIRCRAFT: Me110
TIME ATTACK WAS DELIVERED:
PLACE ATTACK WAS DELIVERED: 25 miles East of Deal
HEIGHT OF ENEMY: Intercepted at 20,000'
ENEMY CASUALTIES: 1 Me.110 (shared with Yellow Section)

General Report. I was leading Green Section on convoy patrol when we sighted several condensation plumes above us. The C.O. led one Flight towards one plume and 'B'

Flight climbed to intercept another. My aircraft was somewhat slower than the other and my Green 2 (Sgt. Plzak) joined Blue Section. Yellow Section managed to head e/a off and it dived towards and underneath us. When I saw it coming I half rolled, closed to 150 yards and opened fire. I continued firing until it entered cloud at about 10,000' when glycol was streaming from the starboard engine, and lots of pieces came off. I then broke away as my ammunition was exhausted. The e/a crashed in the sea and there were no survivors.

DATE: 28/11/40
FLIGHT, SQUADRON: Flight: 'B' Sqdn: 19
NUMBER OF ENEMY AIRCRAFT: Five
TYPE OF ENEMY AIRCRAFT: Me109's
TIME ATTACK WAS DELIVERED: 1530 approx
PLACE ATTACK WAS DELIVERED: 5 miles East of Ramsgate
HEIGHT OF ENEMY: 20,000 feet
ENEMY CASUALTIES: One Me.109.

General Report. Whilst leading 'B' Flight we were informed by Green Leader who was doing rear search that some Me.109 were diving to attack from astern. We immediately went into line astern and turned into them. I climbed with Green 2 and we engaged two of them which were flying in a circle. Mine dived at high speed and was shot at by another Spitfire which appeared to do no damage as e/a pulled out of dive and entered cloud heading towards French Coast. I was able to dimly see e/a and closed into 100 yards and let him have the rest of my ammunition. E/a began issuing black smoke and glycol, which completely obscured its fuselage. Before it crashed into sea off French Coast I noticed one wing gun firing tracer. I had left Duxford at 1435 and landed at 1610.

Leonard Haines was a true hero of the Battle of Britain, and had distinguished himself as an 'Ace'. Tragically his life was cut short as a result of a flying accident at No. 53 Operational Training Unit, on 30 April 1941, while he was instructing. ∎

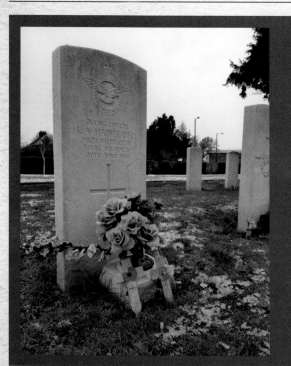

LEONARD ARCHIBALD HAINES DFC

Rank Flying Officer (Pilot Instr.)
Date of Death 30 April 1941
Service No. 40297
Place of Burial Hounslow Cemetery, Plot D. Row B. Grave 2.

Combat Record
(All whilst with No. 19 Squadron)
8 enemy aircraft destroyed
4 enemy aircraft shared destroyed
2 enemy aircraft probables

Source: *Aces High – A tribute to the Most Notable Fighter Pilots of the British and Commonwealth Forces in WWII*, by Christopher Shores and Clive Williams (Grub Street, 1994)

Bandit

Six o'Clock High

Towards the end of spring 1936, a charming young student pilot named Byron Leonard Duckenfield stood on the brink of completing his flying training at No. 10 Flying Training School, Ternhill, near Market Drayton, Shropshire. After some hard grafting, the prize was now in sight, and Duckenfield was keen to obtain his Wings. **Christopher Yeoman** charts his story from fledgling flyer to accomplished fighter pilot.

During the final stages of the course at Ternhill, Byron Duckenfield's flying instructor, a Flight Lieutenant R. E. de T. Vintras, directed him to perform a height climb to 15,000 feet in a Hawker Hart aircraft. The weather was clear and windy, with a cloud cover of 5/10ths at 2,500 feet. The task itself seemed straightforward enough, so, as the youthful pilot from Sheffield trotted off down the runway in his aircraft, he sat unaware of the trouble that lay ahead.

Fifteen minutes after take-off, the keen pupil arrived at the intended height of 15,000 feet and then straightened his aircraft out to enjoy the flight.

Byron Duckenfield picks up the story in his own words:

After some time at this height, I began my descent to return to base, but found that the cloud cover had increased substantially and I was lucky to find a large-enough 'hole' through which to descend until I could get a clear view of the ground. What I found below cloud was a sight to fill the inexperienced pilot, that I was then, with dismay: from one horizon to the other was nothing but bleak, heather-covered moorland. I realised then (too late) that I should have allowed for the strong westerly wind prevailing that day. But now, I was 'lost' and beginning to worry about my remaining fuel.

Finding a fairly busy road through the heather, I followed it south and eventually came to a large town where I spotted a big open space of about 50 acres. Because my fuel was now getting low, I decided to try landing here, and I was lucky when, on final approach, I saw the trolley-bus wires at the last minute, but yet contrived to get over them.

I managed to complete a successful landing without any damage, while scattering a few footballers in my path. They were not in any real danger, because they had seen and heard me coming, and my speed in their vicinity was quite low. Dismounting from the aircraft, I was told that I had landed in Osmaston Park, in the City of Derby.

Thirty-three years later, when I left the Royal Air Force to join Rolls-Royce Aero-engines, I was astonished to find that my office, in the factory adjoining the Park, was less than 200 yards from the spot where I had landed all those years before!

Pipsqueak

Fortunately the remainder of Duckenfield's flying training passed without further incident, and on 8 August 1936 he arrived at Biggin Hill, having been sent to serve with No. 32 Squadron in RAF Fighter Command.

The new recruit soon became accustomed to squadron life and RAF protocol, as he settled into his new posting at Biggin. At this time No. 32 Squadron was equipped with Gloster Gauntlets – single-seater biplane fighters that had a higher rate of performance than anything Duckenfield had flown prior to his posting.

A few years before the start of the war, Sir Henry Tizard, Chairman of the Aeronautical Research Committee, and Air Chief Marshal Sir Hugh Dowding, commanding RAF Fighter Command, with great wisdom and foresight

Below: Portrait of Battle of Britain pilot Byron Duckenfield.

began to develop the RAF's radar system, which was soon to be a crucial part of the war effort. During this time a series of novel experimental flights were orchestrated from Biggin Hill. With No. 32 Squadron, Duckenfield took part in a historic occasion where the testing of a planned interception procedure was conducted. On this encounter, Duckenfield and his companions successfully intercepted an unsuspecting civil aircraft, which had been plotted by Bawdsey Research Station as it flew into Croydon. To avoid suspicion, the fighters continued to fly on course once the interception had been confirmed. The success of this interception, among other results, aided Sir Robert Watson-Watt, the man at the forefront of radar development, in convincing the government to finance a coastal chain of radar stations, which would prove invaluable in the following years.

Reflecting upon this occasion, Duckenfield continues:

The 'Pipsqueak' (A system of ground-based Radio Direction Finding) was a one-minute clock, sited below the throttle lever in the Gauntlet cockpit, and marked in

patrol the Channel between Dover and Dungeness. Flying as No. 2 to Bowler, Duckenfield noted that the weather was fair, with a blue sky and decent visibility. There was broken cumulus cloud over the sea, approximately 4/8ths from 500 to 2,500 feet. Duckenfield continues:

Because of the broken cloud cover, the leader maintained height of 2,000 feet and continued out to sea. So far, we had been entering and emerging from cloud at intervals of a few seconds, but now the cloud seemed to be continuous. We were flying in cloud for two or three minutes at a time with no sign of a break, and the leader began to turn to port, me in close line-astern, presumably to regain the Kent coast.

Now, it is a proven maxim of experienced pilots that one never flies 'by the seat of one's pants' in cloud; one relies absolutely on instruments. But, of course, if flying in formation in cloud, the No. 2 must perforce concentrate exclusively on following the lead aircraft. On this occasion, however, about halfway round, the turn seemed to me to be getting ever steeper and I was having

"A quick glance at the instrument panel confirmed my 'seat of the pants' unease: the gyro compass spinning wildly, unwinding very fast, and the airspeed much too low. Instant conclusion: the aircraft was in an incipient spin and I was still in cloud and had 'lost' the lead aircraft."

four 15-second quadrants. It was the job of the No. 3 in the 'vic' to transmit his call sign continuously during the fourth quadrant. Thus, on the historic occasion mentioned, Pete Brothers was the leader and I was No. 3 (in Gauntlet K5330) transmitting 'Dunbar Blue 6, Dunbar Blue 6 . . .' for 15 seconds each minute.

In 1939, this remarkable development would be put into action as Britain declared itself at war with Germany.

Channel Patrol

A key role for the pilots of Fighter Command in the early stages of the war was the defence of the exposed shipping convoys in the English Channel.

In February 1940, Duckenfield recalls an encounter where he was involved in a Channel patrol with Flying Officer Lance Bowler. After taking off from Biggin Hill in their Hurricanes, Bowler and Duckenfield began to

difficulty in following. A quick glance at the instrument panel confirmed my 'seat of the pants' unease: the gyro compass spinning wildly, unwinding very fast, and the airspeed much too low. Instant conclusion: the aircraft was in an incipient spin and I was still in cloud and had 'lost' the lead aircraft. Immediate recovery action to centralise the rudder bar and throttle back in a shallow dive eventually resulted in stable flight, but with a bare 300 feet height remaining, and I was still in cloud. A steady straight climb from here finally brought me back above cloud at about 3,000 feet, but with no sign of the leader and no response to my R/T calls to him. So I returned alone to base at Biggin Hill and made my report.

Bowler was never seen again; after two days' fruitless search, he was posted 'missing, believed killed'.

In April, a change was in the air for Duckenfield, a change that he was not pleased with in the slightest, as he bid

DAVID PRITCHARD

farewell to No. 32 Squadron and joined No. 74 Squadron, which was equipped with Spitfires.

My time with 74 Squadron was only 24 days, 11 April to 4 May 1940. This was not a happy time because the CO, Squadron Leader White, took an instant dislike to me. To understand — but not forgive — his attitude, I have to explain the background.

It was Air Ministry Policy at that time (it changed later in the war) to post away immediately from his unit any NCO who was granted a commission. So I was torn away from the squadron I had flown with for four years. There was an NCO pilot in 74 Squadron, 'Polly' Flinders, who was commissioned on the same date — 1 April — as me. Flinders was posted from 74 to 32 and I was posted in the other direction, a direct swap. This might explain Squadron Leader White's unreasonable resentment: he had lost an experienced fighter pilot and could not accept that he had gained one equally experienced in return.

To escape this unhappy atmosphere, I had been in 74 Squadron less than two weeks when I responded to a call for volunteers for the Norwegian campaign. Fortunately for me, tragically for those involved, that campaign failed, and I was posted instead to 501 Squadron.

Tragic Crash

Six days after Duckenfield had joined No. 501 Squadron, he was involved in the tragic crash of a Bristol Bombay

transport aircraft, which claimed the lives of three squadron members and the Bombay crew, as well as injuring six others.

Following the German invasion of Holland and Belgium two days before, 501 Squadron moved on 11 May 1940 from Tangmere in Hampshire to France. I had been posted to the squadron only three days before the move, so, being a 'new boy', I was not allowed to fly a Hurricane across to France, even though I had many more hours' experience on this type than any other of the squadron pilots. Instead, I went as a passenger with some of the squadron ground crew and a few other 'new' pilots in a Bristol Bombay.

Arriving over the destination airfield at Betheniville (near Epernay), the Bombay pilot approached to land but aborted the landing, being too high on final approach at the airfield boundary. Going round again, the pilot made a second attempt, but it was apparent to me, looking out of a fuselage window, that the aircraft was still much too high at about 200 feet above the airfield.

What happened next was learned afterwards from eyewitness friends on the ground. The aircraft was at about 200 feet, too high on final approach. When the engines were throttled back, the nose of the aircraft rose quickly to near vertical; the aircraft stalled and began a tail-slide, falling rapidly backward. Just before impact with the ground, the fuselage levelled and the aircraft hit the ground flat.

The fact that the aircraft had levelled just before impact saved most of those on board from fatal injury, but there were still five fatalities. These had been seated under the centre section of the mainplane (it was a high-wing monoplane), and they had been crushed by the collapse of the centre section. I was fortunate; I had been sitting between two of the dead, but had changed mid-flight to another position.

I was fortunate again a few minutes later when I regained consciousness in the collapsed ruin of the aircraft to discover the blade of a salvaging saw approaching dangerously close to my leg. It stopped when I shouted and I was eventually cut free and taken to a casualty station at a chateau in Epernay.

After a few days on penicillin and Guinness, I was transported by ambulance train to Dieppe and by ship to Newhaven, finally to Roehampton Hospital. So, on my first visit to France, my feet literally 'never touched the ground!'

Into Battle

After recovering from his injuries, Duckenfield returned to England, and in July was soon back in the air with No. 501 Squadron. On 29 July, flying as Green 2, Duckenfield took off in his Hurricane from 501's forward base at Hawkinge and began to patrol the morning sky with his section. Shortly after they had become airborne, an emergency order from control directed them to Dover, which was under heavy air attack. Duckenfield remembers the event well:

I noted the sky seemed full of aircraft; Dover Harbour was being dive-bombed by about thirty Ju87 Stuka aircraft, pursued by many Hurricanes and Spitfires. We joined the hunt and found the Ju87 to be an easy prey. Yes, they were very difficult to follow down in their steep 70-degree dive, but when they levelled out to scoot home across the water, it was so easy, firing from slightly above and astern, to bring fire to bear with accuracy merely by using the water splashes around the target to correct one's aim. The Luftwaffe lost at least eight Ju87 aircraft that day, and, after more punishing losses in the following week, the Ju87 was withdrawn from further attacks on the UK.

15 August 1940 saw the most intensive fighting in the Battle of Britain to date. Frustrated by the Luftwaffe's lack of success, Goering launched his air force to concentrate its attacks on RAF airfields. The conflict was bitter, but the RAF prevailed in gaining the day's victory. No. 501 Squadron fared particularly well throughout its engagements with the enemy, Duckenfield included. On an early patrol Pilot Officer Duckenfield claimed a Dornier Do 215 as a 'probable', but on a later patrol, when flying near Tunbridge Wells, another Dornier Do 215 crashed in flames at Bletchinglye Farm, after being struck by Duckenfield's guns.

During the long hot summer of 1940, Duckenfield continued to fly operational sorties with No. 501 Squadron, and, on 8 September, he tangled with the Luftwaffe's finest fighter aircraft, the Messerschmitt 109.

```
Combat Report Excerpt:
29 July 1940

Enemy a/c first seen diving on Dover Harbour out of the sun, i.e. from ESE. Our
position was then 8,000' N. of Dover. Squadron had to go round to the W. of Dover to
avoid barrage. Anti-aircraft fire burst within 300 x of me, so I broke away to the
right in the direction of Folkestone. I flew out about 10 miles and saw Ju 87's
diving vertically on Dover Harbour and breaking away to the South at about 2000'
I was then at 4000' and dived down on a Ju 87 which was being attacked by another
Hurricane. I do not know if it was damaged. I then looked round and saw a continuous
stream of E/A flying South from Dover. I did a quarter attack on one E/A, opening
fire about 300 x. When I had closed to about 150 x, another Hurricane came in between
the target and myself, so I ceased firing. The other Hurricane closed to about 50 x
and I saw the E/A burst into flames and dived into the sea. I then broke away and
returned to base.
```

(The use of 'x' in the above combat narrative was used in the handwritten report. It is likely to mean yards.)

Weaving back and forth behind his squadron, through towering cumulus cloud as 'tail end Charlie', Duckenfield searched his surroundings for any telltale signs of enemy aircraft. Maintaining height at 15,000 feet somewhere between Folkestone and Dover, Duckenfield continued to weave his aircraft behind the leading Hurricanes until suddenly out of nowhere he caught sight of a bright flash in his rear-view mirror. Quickly warning the squadron over the R/T, Duckenfield yelled 'Bandit, six o'clock high!' and pulled hard on his control column to evade the 109's guns. Duckenfield pulled a max-rate turn in an attempt to get behind his attacker, but by the time the manoeuvre was completed the 109 was diving safely into cloud.

I dived to follow, emerging below cloud at about 1,500 feet, and was lucky enough to see the enemy aircraft streaking away south-east ahead of me. Following at maximum speed, in and out of cloud base, I tried to close

My year in AFDU was one of the most enjoyable and rewarding of my RAF service. As a very junior officer, I was fortunate to be sent to such an interesting and challenging post, where, in the space of fourteen months, I flew many different aircraft types and gained so much valuable experience.

On 24 September 1941, Byron Duckenfield was awarded the Air Force Cross, and the following month he took command of No. 66 Squadron at RAF Perranporth. In February 1942, Duckenfield's leadership qualities were needed elsewhere, so he was sent to No. 615 Squadron stationed at RAF Fairwood Common, and, a month later, he led the squadron to the Far East. In December, after leading the squadron on an offensive sortie over Magwe airfield, Duckenfield was forced to land his aircraft in a shallow creek because he was losing his airscrew. Being 300 miles away from friendly territory, Duckenfield soon

"I saw some rounds strike but by then it was time to turn back and abandon the chase. On landing at Gravesend, the ground crew pointed out – to my great surprise – the chain of large bullet holes covering the length of the port wing."

up to within firing range but, when almost halfway across the Straits, the best I could manage was a long burst at about 300 yards.

Thumbing the gun button, Duckenfield awoke the Hurricane's guns and unleashed a decent burst of ammunition at the German fighter.

I saw some rounds strike but by then it was time to turn back and abandon the chase. On landing at Gravesend, the ground crew pointed out – to my great surprise – the chain of large bullet holes covering the length of the port wing.

Several days later Duckenfield received a break from the front line when he was posted to RAF Northolt to serve as a test pilot at the Air Fighting Development Unit (AFDU). It was here that Duckenfield performed various roles, such as testing new Allied aircraft, captured enemy aircraft, and instructing bomber aircraft crews. The now accomplished fighter pilot from Sheffield found this period especially beneficial to his career. Duckenfield concludes:

became a prisoner of the Japanese. After a difficult two and a half years in Rangoon Jail, Duckenfield returned home in May 1945. After a long and respectable career in the RAF, Group Captain Duckenfield retired on 28 June 1969, having obtained a wealth of experience from his labours and having achieved a great deal of success in the service of his country. ■

Left:
Byron Duckenfield in 2005.

Polish Disobedience

"Stop that Polish chatter and steer two – three – zero...*Repeat Please*...I say again, two – three – zero...*Repeat Please*...For crying out loud!...*Repeat Please*...Two – three – zero ...*Repeat Please*...*Repeat Please*...Now just shut up the lot of you and follow me, unless you're blind as well as – Oh God, streuth!"

It is one of the most memorable moments in the Battle of Britain feature film. Polish pilots, on a training flight, seem unable to hear the instructions of their RAF formation leader, as he orders them to steer away from danger. This episode may have been subject to a little dramatic licence; however it was founded in fact. On 30 August 1940, Polish pilots of No. 303 Squadron were on a training flight when enemy aircraft were spotted, and they did engage their enemy, with some success. Aviation archaeologist **Julian Evan-Hart** pieces together the fate of one enemy aircraft that fell to either Polish disobedience or a lust for revenge – probably both.

O n Friday 30 August 1940, 'sharks mouth' emblazoned twin-engined Messerschmitt 110s took off once more from Le Mans Abbeville. At the controls of the one marked M8+MM was 27-year-old Oberfeldwebel Georg Anthony. He had already become a very seasoned and experienced veteran and, together with Heinrich Nordmeier as his radio operator and gunner, had actively participated in the French campaign. In the Battle of France Anthony had led several daring and well-executed attacks on French aeroplanes, shooting down several Morane-Saulnier fighters. Georg Anthony was frequently to be found embroiled in some frantic aerial combats; and as well as achieving a reputation, he appeared to be well on the way to becoming one of the war's earliest ZG76 (Zerstörergeschwader 76) aces. However, the fickle fortunes of war would deny him achieving this status.

On this day his Messerschmitt was to act as one of the many escort fighters for the Heinkel He111s of Kampfgeschwader 53. From approximately 1415 hours an estimated 300 enemy aeroplanes were approaching the

Thames Estuary and Kent Coast. From these areas they divided into smaller groups and proceeded inland. Attacks were made on Debden, Biggin Hill, and other significant aerodromes. One group of KG53 Heinkels and their Me110 escorts, initially heading for Radlett aerodrome, became detached. One of this group, a Heinkel 111, was shot down at Hunsdon in Hertfordshire. This group penetrated as far inland as Luton, where they found and bombed the Vauxhall Motor Works. The Heinkels of KG53 released fifty-nine bombs onto the factory and surrounding area of Luton. The Engineering Section of the works was very badly hit; one direct hit killed seven people sheltering beneath a stairway. In Luton a total of twenty people were killed, one hundred and seventy four injured, of which forty-nine were serious. Despite the extensive damage the plant was back in production within six days. It took some time longer, though, for Bomb Disposal to clear and render safe the many UXBs that lay in the district.

The Raiders Head for Home

Leaving their target shrouded in smoke and dust the raiding force turned east and headed towards the Thames Estuary and home. Two aircraft of the Vauxhall raid were lost on the way to the target. One fell near Kimpton, Hertfordshire the other, also an Me110 which was coded M8+BM, crashed into a sewage works at Enfield in Essex.

One eyewitness to this attack was living in Stevenage, Hertfordshire, at the time and said, 'You could see the German aeroplanes, they were ever so high. They looked like mere specks in the blue sky, if you listened carefully you could just hear faint sounds of machine gun fire.' Other witnesses spoke of hearing the ominous fluctuating drone of the approaching German formation. Another eyewitness residing in Welwyn Garden City actually saw Nordmeier bale out from the stricken aeroplane.

Combat

On a training flight in the area at this time, No. 303 Squadron from Northolt literally stumbled upon the enemy aeroplanes. They took no time in getting stuck into the escorts and their bomb-laden Heinkels. Opposite is the combat report of Flying Officer Ludwik 'Pazkiewicz' (sometimes written Paszkiewicz). The combat report records his victim as either a Dornier 17 or a Dornier 215, but it was in fact the Me110 flown by Oberfeldwebel Georg Anthony.

COMBAT REPORT

F/O L. Pazkiewicz (Polish)
Date: 30.8.40
Flight, Squadron: Flight B Sqdn 303 (Polish)
Number of Enemy aircraft: about 130
Type of Enemy aircraft: Do.17 or 215 & Me.110
Time Attack was delivered: 1635
Place Attack was delivered: St. Albans
Height of Enemy: 14,000 – 9,000 ft
Enemy Casualties: One Do.17 or 215. destroyed
Our Casualties – Aircraft: Nil
Personnel: Nil

General Report

I was Green 1 flying Hurricane RF.V. I took off at 1615 and flew with 5 others of 'B' flight to St. Albans at 9,000 feet on exercise to intercept 6 Blenheims. At about 1635 I saw fire on the ground and shells bursting at my altitude, and a strong enemy formation in two tiers in echelon at about 14,000 feet flying from starboard. I saw some of our fighters among them. I said to Apany leader 'Bandits 10 o'clock', but received no reply. I made towards the enemy. The flight remained behind me. I waggled my wings, and then saw at the same altitude as myself an E/A banking towards me. When he was almost head on, he saw me and went into a steep dive. I followed, and, as he pulled out, I fired from directly behind a burst at 250 yards at the fuselage. Overtaking him, I fired a long burst at 100 to 20 yards at the starboard engine from underneath. The engine stopped and burst into flames. I broke off. As another Hurricane UC.J. went in to attack, I saw a parachute leave E/A. Enemy dived. I followed down and gave E/A a short burst, though I realised immediately that it was not necessary. E/A crashed and exploded. I regained height, and, being unable to see my flight, I returned to Northolt.

II./Zerstörergeschwader 76

Lfd. Nr.	Ort und Tag des Verlustes / Feindflug ja oder nein	Staffel usw.	Dienstgrad Dienst-stellung	Vorname	Familienname, Truppenteil, Nr. der Erkennungsmarke	Geburts-		
						tag	ort	kreis
1	2	3	4	5	6	7	8	9
1	20 km N.W. London 30.8.1940 ja	4./Z.G. 76	Hptm. Staffel-kapitän	Heinz	Wagner 4./Z.G. 76 Stammkomp. L.K.S. Dresden Nr. 98	7. 1. 09.	Dan-zig	
2	20 km N.W. London 30.8.1940 ja	4./Z.G. 76	Stabs-feldw. Bord-funker	Adolf	Schmidt 4./Z.G. 76 8/53547	14. 3. 07.	Ernst-thal Krs. Sonne-berg	
3	15 km N.W. London 30.8.1940 ja	4./Z.G. 76	Ofw. Flugzeug-führer	Georg	Anthony 4./Z.G. 76 B 65 141 Nr.7	29. 5. 13.	Ber-lin	
4	15 km N.W. London 30.8.1940 ja	4./Z.G. 76	Uffz. Bord-funker 19.7.12 b. Dab.	Heinrich	Nordmeier 4./Z.G. 76 75/ 5/54 F.B.K.	■■■	■■■	
5	Gegend Calais 30.8.1940 ja	6./Z.G. 76	Hptm. Staffel-kapitän	Heinz	Nacke 6./Z.G. 76 B 65 143 Nr. 1	■■■		
6	Gegend Calais 30.8.1940 ja	6./Z.G. 76	Stabs-Feldw.	Alfred	Kühne 6./Z.G. 76 53543/9	■■■		
7	2.9.1940 N.O. London ja	Stab II./Z.G. 76	Oblt. Flug-zeugfhr.	Karl	Urede Stab II./Z.G.76 B 65 140 Nr.4	■■■		

*) Abkürzungen: K. = Kopf, H. = Hals, Br. = Brust, Ba. = Bauch, R. = Rücken, I.A. = Unter Arm (I.G. = Infanteriegeschß, H.Gr. = Handgranatenverletzung, Cls.V. = Kampfliefloengh

**) Hierzu rechnen auch Verwundungen und Verletzungen durch Kampfe Gewalt infolge feindlicher Einwirkung, durch Verschüttung usw.

Right: King George VI talks to Polish pilots of No. 303 Squadron. Left to right: S/L Urbanowicz, F/Lt R. S. Forbes, F/Lt Ludwik Paszkiewicz (killed in action the next day) and F/Lt Walery Zak.

Right: King George VI talks to Polish pilots of No. 303 Squadron. Left to right: S/L Urbanowicz, F/Lt R. S. Forbes, F/Lt Ludwik Paszkiewicz (killed in action the next day) and F/Lt Walery Zak.

There is undoubtedly a mistake in the combat report with respect to the lettering of the other Hurricane Paszkiewicz mentions. It is likely to have been US-J (i.e. No. 56 Squadron) and not UC-J. It is believed that the second attacker was Pilot Officer B. J. Wicks of No. 56 Squadron based at North Weald.

Ludwik Paszkiewicz would go on to make further claims during the Battle of Britain, ending up with a total of six enemy aircraft destroyed. But he would not survive the air battle. On 27 September 1940 Hurricane L1696, coded RF-M, smashed into the ground at Crowhurst Farm, Borough Green, Kent. The young pilot killed in the impact was Ludwik Paszkiewicz. Many years later aviation archaeologists were to excavate the impact point of L1696. Here they recovered numerous artefacts including a propeller blade that was subsequently donated to the Sikorsky Museum in London. Ludwik Paszkiewicz is buried in Northwood cemetery.

Witnesses

Returning to 30 August 1940, far below, villagers and farm workers witnessed a thrilling dogfight, involving numerous aeroplanes wheeling and diving; now the

Right:
Ludwik Paszkiewicz rests with other Polish colleagues at Northwood cemetery, London.

machine-gun fire was much louder. One eyewitness counted twenty-seven German aeroplanes in formation, with three RAF fighters attacking them. A Mrs Sharnbrook had a superb view of the combat being played out above her; she remarked how the 'British fighters looked like angry wasps going in to attack'. Frequently there would be a sharp flash and glint of light as the bright sun reflected off the cockpits of friend and foe alike.

A Police Constable Pavett had watched the entire dogfight from a distance and as it got louder and louder he placed his wife and family in the garden air-raid shelter.

Black Smoke Lines the Summer Sky

The 'twin-engined bomber' that Ludwik Paszkiewicz had singled out near Welwyn Garden City was the Me110 being flown by Georg Anthony. Trying desperately to shake off his determined attacker Anthony dived away sharply. Twisting and turning at full throttle the Messerschmitt could not lose itself from the sight of the pursuing Pole. Paszkiewicz opened fire and small fragments of fuselage became detached from his Messerschmitt amid a series of flashes and puffs of white smoke. Banking sharply, a furious and accurate burst of gunfire caused the starboard wing tip of Anthony's Messerschmitt to disintegrate. This ripped away and fluttered back past the attacking Hurricane. Unceasingly the De Wilde ammunition from the Hurricane flashed and sparked as it hit M8+MM. The .303 rounds either punched small neat holes or great paint-splintered ragged holes, as M8+MM jinked from side to side through which the air stream whistled and shrieked. Above the screaming noise from the port engine Anthony and Nordmeier could hear the clattering sounds from damaged and detaching sections of their aeroplane. The starboard engine of the Messerschmitt was now badly damaged, and from it large gouts of flame and black smoke began to line the summer sky. Surprisingly despite being seriously damaged Anthony still managed to keep his aeroplane in horizontal flight.

Paszkiewicz then saw another Hurricane draw alongside him and also fire on 'his' target. After this attack Nordmeier jettisoned the rear cockpit canopy and baled out over the Hertfordshire countryside.

Plummeting Earthwards

On the ground below, stopping work to watch the dogfight were Jack Marshall and Alf Symons. Up above they watched the final attack delivered on what they concluded was an 'already seriously done-for Jerry.' Almost immediately afterwards the German aircraft rolled over, assumed an inverted position, and began to plummet earthwards with a terrifying scream. Picking up incredible speed further sections detached and fluttered away lost briefly from sight in the rushing smoke plume. The tail unit briefly swung sideways and then snapped off and spun away having been under the pressure of terrific forces. The tattered remains of M8+MM continued to fall down through the bright summer sky with a terrible whining scream. Just before impact the broken Messerschmitt seemed to level out, and then it smashed through a row of mature elm trees. These huge trees sheared off the remains

JULIAN EVAN-HART

of the wings outboard of each engine, shattered the fuselage, and totally broke off the cockpit structure. In a flurry of shattered wood, twigs, leaves, and smoke the remainder of the wreckage crashed through into a corner of a field bordering Claggybottom Lane. The nose section compressed in a second as it tore into the ground instantly ramming compressed clay three feet up each cannon gun barrel. The two hot engines then hit the ground ripping off their propeller bosses and shearing off some blades before punching eight feet into the stone-laden clay. These engines took the nose and part of the cockpit section down with them. One man standing over half a mile away actually said he felt the vibration of impact through his feet. Immediately, the Messerschmitt exploded and a huge ball of orange flame shot up followed by a thick billowing black smoke plume. Just over a thousand feet above the shattered tranquillity of this English countryside

scene Wicks, pilot of the second Hurricane, performed a victory roll. Georg Anthony the Me110 pilot was to stay inside until impact. Had he been killed in the attacks by Paszkiewicz or Wicks, was he only wounded, or simply could not release the canopy due to damage? We shall never know.

PC Pavett watched a body tumble from the sky until a parachute opened at a low height and it drifted down across the fields near Tallents Farm. He went off in the direction he assumed the parachutist to have come down in and found Nordmeier, who had hit the ground heavily and whose spine was broken in several places. PC Pavett reported that he was a tall blond-haired fellow; still alive, with a large bloodied gash on his forehead, but barely conscious. Being nervous that the German could be shamming his consciousness PC Pavett disarmed him, released his harness and had him conveyed to Kimpton on a stretcher. Amongst some of the items 'liberated' from the pockets of the lucky-to-be-alive radio operator was a quantity of British-manufactured cigarettes. One wonders if these cigarettes may have originated from the supplies left behind during the Dunkirk Evacuation. When Nordmeier arrived at Kimpton he was attended by a Dr Probyn and then conveyed by ambulance to a nearby searchlight unit situated in Whitwell.

Crash Investigation

Having completed the task of handing Nordmeier over to the military authorities PC Pavett, along with four members of the Home Guard, decided to make his way to the crash site. As he neared the elm trees he could see a large number of people had gathered next to the smoking crater. These included another member of the constabulary and some more Home Guard members, who were doing their best to cordon off the crater from sightseers and souvenir hunters.

When the flames and smoke had subsided, partially as a result of a Fire Brigade team in attendance, a crater could be seen. This was some twenty feet across and five feet deep. From the depths protruded a mass of mangled

Below right:
Funeral of Georg
Anthony at Hitchin,
September 1940.

metal, wiring, and about six inches of one buried propeller blade. It would seem that as the remains of M8+MM had only penetrated some eight feet into the flinty clay of the field, the impact velocity had been considerably reduced by collision with the trees. From inside the crater could also be seen the bloodied and tattered remains of the lower half of Georg Anthony's body. Scattered around the crater were large sections of wing structure and fuselage fragments.

A Grisly Aftermath

Looking up into the shattered top section of an elm tree someone noticed a large section of uniformed torso from which blood had dripped down the bark. Also lying in the vicinity to the horror of locals lay a flying boot complete with a foot inside, and a head minus its scalp. The scalp of ginger-coloured hair was recovered later. Tattered fragments of uniform and more minor human remains lay scattered across the lane and the adjacent field. Near to the hedge one lucky souvenir seeker is reported to have picked up a pack of coloured pencils. Another person, perhaps a member of the constabulary, caught a man making off with Georg Anthony's side-arm pistol that he had found in the lane. Later that afternoon, with the road sealed off, PC Pavett began discreetly collecting the human remains from within and around the crater. These included the quite macabre sight of two clenched severed hands in a nearby hedgerow. He assumed they were in such a condition due to the pilot strenuously pulling on the control column. Collecting as much as he could find, which came to nearly three-quarters of a grain sack, he placed the remains at the bottom of his garden. Here they remained for several days until attracting so many blowflies he decided to convey them in a tea chest to Hitchin for military funeral preparations. PC Pavett later confirmed that as far as he knew no identity tag was found with the remains.

Back at the crash scene a photographer from the *Herts Pictorial* newspaper had arrived, and took a considerable amount of exposures. These included some posed shots with Home Guard members around the wreckage. The newspaper reported that due to the violent nature of the

JULIAN EVAN-HART

crash it was not possible to ascertain what type of enemy aeroplane this was. It was noted that around the crater's edge and also in the lane were found some shredded sections of flight map. The newspaper reports indicate this is evidence that the pilot attempted to destroy the map as he fell. In addition to this it was stated a partially deployed parachute was evidence that he had made some attempt to vacate the stricken aeroplane. While both indeed could be true it was more likely due to the violence of the impact.

One week after the crash the pitiful remains of Georg Anthony were accorded a military funeral, the cortège passing through the streets of Hitchin. His coffin, draped in a swastika flag, was placed on a wheeled carriage and pulled through the crowd-lined streets and led to the cemetery. It is recorded that the RAF attended the funeral; whether this included Paszkiewicz and Wicks this author has not been able to establish. One hopes it was them attending to pay their respects to a gallant but fallen foe. The remains of Georg Anthony still rests in Hitchin cemetery to this day; unlike so many of his Luftwaffe colleagues he was not exhumed and re-buried at Cannock Chase in the 1960s. In fact a few feet away lies the body of Wolfgang Eurl who was killed in the Heinkel 111 crash at Bendish some months later in April 1941.

For days after the crash people visited the site to look for souvenirs; items so recovered ranged from small twisted pieces of alloy to live cannon shells. However, this author is sure that other fascinating finds were made along the hedgerows by keen-eyed searchers. How many such items have been lost or thrown out since? Who knows if Georg Anthony's identity tag or wrist watch were indeed found at the time, and now reside in dusty brown envelopes in a neglected attic! Finally, a Queen Mary low-loader vehicle arrived and assisted in the removal of all large surface wreckage. Three days later a young lad climbed to the top of one of the elm trees to grab a piece of the Messerschmitt that was still stuck up there. As he tore it down he could see that it was riddled with bullet holes. Such souvenir gathering also had its advantages, some quite ironic. Such as Peter Stokes a local lad who managed to raise five shillings and seven pence from selling pieces to family and friends, later donated to the Spitfire fund. Perhaps the most remarkable souvenir to be taken was

that removed by a Mr Ansell soon afterwards. Visiting the crash site on the evening it happened he managed to take home a huge section of fuselage bearing the Balkan Kreuz. He retained this for many years until it was sold to a passing scrap merchant. Mr Ansell later wrote, 'On the afternoon of Friday 30 August 1940 a German plane was shot down by our fighters and crashed at Claggybottom near Kimpton. At that time I lived at Diamond End and went to the scene within an hour of the crash. One of the crew managed to bale out and was captured but one was killed. I saw part of his body hanging in a tree. In the evening I returned to the scene and took part of the fuselage, which included the "Iron Cross" which I kept as a souvenir for many years. On that evening, as the strength of the summer sun ebbed, a strange creaking noise emanated from the depths of the crater, even after several hours the engines of M8+MM were still cooling down.'

68 Years On

The landowner excavated the buried remains of M8+MM in 1982. Amongst items recovered were both engines, both being in excellent condition, although, as to be expected, the starboard example bore evidence of fire damage. It also bore some bullet strike marks on the casing. Impacted clay was rammed into every engineered crevice on the engines and both had adherent orange-coloured clay. Orange-coloured because the heat from each engine had literally fired the surrounding clay. Both undercarriage assemblies were also found, along with much-compressed radiator, tubing, rubber pipes, manufacturer's plates, both propeller bosses, and masses of compressed airframe. One of the propeller bosses has a small section of propeller blade protruding from it; on this can be seen traces of red paint. The forward firing 20mm cannons were found still in their shrouding exploder tubes. The force of the impact could also be seen as their breech mechanisms were buckled and split. The landowner was also extremely fortunate to locate a splendid brown, blue, and gold colour enamel engine badge from the Niedersachsige Motoren Werke at Braunschweig. This showed the NMW logo with a walking lion above it, a truly evocative little artefact relating back to the height of the Battle of Britain.

Of the crash site today there is little evidence at all; the odd green or grey painted fragment of airframe is occasionally visible in the plough soil from the roadside. Of the once magnificent elms that lined the field and lane there remains just rotten ivy-clad stumps, barely discernible amongst the roadside vegetation. Several years ago this author checked one of these stumps and there in the leaf mould was a large lump of Daimler Benz engine casting complete with exhaust valve. Further rummaging around revealed other sections, some from the cowling and pieces of corroded skinning. Julian Evan-hart recalls, 'I wondered if I had discovered the long forgotten stash of a 1940s schoolboy. And somewhere nearby, maybe, just a few inches under the leaf mould, the roots of a nettle twist and curl around a bent and twisted Luftwaffe pilot's badge. So what was then a quiet leafy lane with thick hedges in 1940 is now a windswept open lane across arable farmland. In sixty-eight years the scenery has changed dramatically, particularly attributable to Dutch elm disease.

I have always wondered how many commuting workers, or others, or even locals now who travel up and down this little back lane to their homes even know what violence occurred along here on that hot summer afternoon back in 1940. But hopefully there are a few like me, who for curiosity's sake and research purposes still go and look over the bleak fields and nettle-filled lane edge. Perhaps they too may close their eyes for a few seconds and imagine shouting voices from across the fields, the acrid smell of burning metal, combined with the irritated calls of a Yellowhammer, and think of a summer tranquillity brutally interrupted some six decades before.' ∎

Left: The brown, blue, and gold enamel engine badge from the stricken ME110.

Left: The grave of German pilot Georg Anthony at Hitchin cemetery, amidst Commonwealth War Grave Commission graves and civilian graves.

Reclaiming a 'Missing' Hurricane

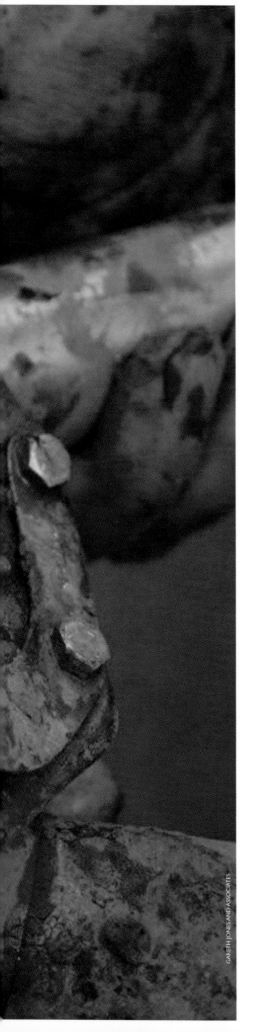

On 5 November 1940, during a patrol over Dorset at 20,000 feet, Polish pilot Jozef Jeka, while flying Hurricane V7535, would cross swords with none other than Jagdgeschwader 2's Major Helmut Wick, who was at the time the Luftwaffe's highest-scoring individual. **Julian Evan-Hart** recounts the story of the engagement and the search for Jeka's 'missing' Hurricane.

On Tuesday, 5 November 1940, just five days after the date that is now said to mark the end of the Battle of Britain, daytime aerial combats were still raging around the east and south coasts and deep into mainland Britain. But the Luftwaffe was making a clearly identifiable and tactical conversion to a night offensive that would be known as the Blitz. The weather on that far-off November day had started rather chilly, but overall conditions were an improvement from the previous week or so. Consequently, Luftwaffe fighter sweeps over southern England came in fast and furious. They included the Me 109s of Jagdgeschwader 26, carrying single bombs. Perhaps some people considered the irony of the fact that the day on which bombs were being dropped on them from above was the very date that was synonymous with explosives of the past. For one young Polish pilot, the date of 5 November would, for the rest of his life, always be associated with luck and a terrifying near-death experience in the skies over Dorset, England.

Jozef Jeka, who was born on 6 April 1917, was just 23 years old when he arrived at Saint-Eval on 2 September to join No. 238 Squadron as a Sergeant Pilot. The badge of No. 238 Squadron was the three-headed Hydra, a creature that, according to Greek mythology, was most difficult to kill. Just thirteen days later, Jeka shot down a Messerschmitt Bf 110, and on 26 September he claimed two Heinkel 111s. One day later, on 27 September, he continued to prove his determination and keen aggression when he shared in the destruction of another Me110, and on 7 October he would bring down a Junkers 88.

Left: Hawker Aircraft manufacturing plate, showing clearly V7535.

Classic 'Bounce'

The use of the term 'cross swords' above is perhaps not quite correct, because the by-then famous and somewhat ebullient Wick quite simply, efficiently, and quickly shot Jeka's Hurricane out of the wartorn skies of Britain, giving the Polish pilot no chance at all to respond. This was an example of a classic 'bounce' performed by JG2. Within two minutes, four of No. 238 Squadron's Hurricanes would be shot down. As JG2 came in fast above and slightly to the side of the Hurricanes, the leading Me109s started to open fire. Behind the Hurricanes the pale blue sky was instantly threaded with thin white spiralling tracer trail. As soon as their pilots realised that they were under attack, the Hurricanes separated all over the place. They twisted and banked away both to the side and downwards, but the Hurricanes had little time before the attack quickly turned into selected individual combats.

IMAGES VIA JULIAN EVAN-HART

Two RAF fighters began to stream white and black mixed smoke trails and spun earth-wards, as did a third. It looked as if the 'Hydra' was not that difficult to kill after all. Like the others, Jeka had virtually no chance to take further evasive action before his attacker, 25-year-old Major Helmut Wick, closed in and lined him up in his Revi gun sight. Wrenching the Me109 over to follow his target, he

gripped the control column as he flicked up the gun cover and opened fire at the fleeing Hurricane. Wavering streams of 7.92 MG17 rounds and the slower velocity thudding 20mm cannon shells briefly found Jeka's Hurricane. The smaller MG17 rounds pierced through the taut-doped rear fuselage and tail-fin fabric, some striking and splintering the internal wooden framework. The larger 20mm shells mainly passed straight through the fuselage, ripping away strips and tatters of fabric on their exit. Jeka could hear the rounds hitting home. Some of the high-explosive cannon shells momentarily found more robust metal obstructions inside the fuselage and detonated with blinding white flashes, severing control cables and blasting away sections of distorted tubing with larger sheets of fabric attached. Instantly, wind shrieked through the tattered airframe. The Luftwaffe ace's bullets and shells spattered their way along the fuselage of Jeka's Hurricane, smashing into its wing roots, bursting a retracted main tyre and then punching toward the Rolls Royce engine. Several MG17 bullets pierced the thin aluminium cowling covers, leaving circular holes as they went on to impact on the hard engine casing. Others seemed to skid across, leaving thin tears surrounded by areas of flaked paint. Several loud and bright explosions in the same area were indicative that HE 20mm cannon shells had also reached the engine area. In just over a second the Hurricane was turned into a smoking tattered mass, and then fire broke out. Gouts of flames and thick burning oil created a thin plume of oily brown and white smoke that trailed out far behind the Hurricane. With the flames coming inside the cockpit section, Jeka flipped the canopy and bailed out while over the village of Sturminster Marshall in Dorset. Drifting down, he watched the results of the carnage, as smoke trails and falling aircraft seemed to be all around him. Wick peeled over to starboard and attempted to rejoin a few of his scattered JG2 colleagues, briefly looking for yet more targets before they had to high tail it back over to France, because the Me109s had severe operational fuel limitations.

Owing to the high level of pilot attrition in the dangerous skies of 1940, fate would turn its tables on Helmut Wick, who just twenty-three days later was killed when his Messerschmitt Bf 109E-2 was shot down into the sea near the Isle of Wight.

Impact

The Hurricane V7535 flipped over to one side and started its descent earthwards. The entire front and the cockpit area were bathed in orange flames, streaking back well beyond the tail section, and the smoke trail was now darker and more defined, as the fuselage and tail section also caught fire. As it plummeted down, flaming sections of fabric detached in the slip stream and spiralled downwards, each leaving its own smaller smoke trail. The fire-engulfed RAF fighter plane was now heading down almost vertically, giving the appearance of a smoke-tailed comet. It struck an agricultural field on Manor Farm at Sturminster Marshall and exploded. Upon impact, the wooden propeller blades were snapped off at their roots and further splintered as their black laminate covering shattered from the weight of the engine as it drove them into the ground. However, one yellow-painted propeller blade tip ripped off and stuck upright in the soil some distance away. The wings were instantly smashed off, as the heavy engine and boss punched through the sandy soil, crumpling and dragging down the attached cockpit area and tangled fuselage wreckage to a depth of 20 feet. The propeller boss itself had been sheared away by the forces of impact at a depth of some 10 feet. The eight Browning .303 machine guns were instantly torn from their mounts, smashing into the ground like darts with barrels bending and breech blocks splitting wide open, scattering twisted sections of .303 ammunition belts everywhere. The small explosion was immediately followed by a large column of dark smoke, rising up slightly but soon drifting across the fields in the afternoon breeze. Ammunition began to 'crackle and pop' as a fire began to take hold, but the sandy nature of the soil meant that much oil and fuel seeped away and the fire, thus starved of accelerant, soon died down. The RAF recovery crew was quickly in attendance, clearing up the site, but, as the pilot had bailed out, there seemed little point in making much of this now ever familiar occasion, so they concentrated on recovering the shallow impacted armament, picking up the scattered surface debris and in-filling the small crater. Locals scoured the crash site and removed some small fragments, and slowly the slight depression that remained was ploughed out and levelled. Sixty-six harvests would come and go on this field before anyone would even find, let alone examine, the precise impact point of Hurricane V7535 again. Of the three other Hurricanes shot down in this particular combat by the pilots of JG2, Pilot Officer

Jeka's RAF Career

JOZEF JEKA went on to earn considerable distinction with the RAF through the rest of the war, awarded the Cross of Valour and three Bars, a Virtuti Militari (Poland's highest military decoration), the Distinguished Flying Medal and the Silver Cross of Merit with Swords. By 1944 he had accounted for seven enemy aircraft destroyed and one shared destroyed, and three damaged, but would fall victim to the enemy on 21 May 1944. He managed to evade capture in France and returned to operational flying in September 1944.

Post-war, Jeka was the first ever Polish pilot to fly at Mach 2, but sadly he was to be killed later, in an A26 crash while participating in clandestine missions for the Central Intelligence Agency in America.

Jozef Jeka's DFM recommendation, 28 July 1941.

'This Sergeant fought last summer with an English Squadron destroying five enemy aircraft, probably destroyed two more and shared in the destruction of another. With 306 (Polish) Squadron he has taken part in many offensive sweeps over France in the course of which he has destroyed one enemy aircraft and damaged another. At all times he has shown the greatest courage and determination to inflict losses on the enemy.'

VIA JULIAN EVAN-HART

Left: Jeka with fellow pilots.

This page, clockwise:
The first scrapes are taken from the impact point of Jeka's Hurricane; Jozef Jeka's control column sees the light of day after nearly seven decades. Steve Vizard (on left) and Gareth Jones; further scrapes.

ALL AIRCRAFT RECOVERY IMAGES BY GARETH JONES AND ASSOCIATES

Considine bailed out near Shapwick, Pilot Officer Rohacek crash-landed at Tarrant Hinton, and Sergeant Pearson crash landed at Tarrant Monkton – all locations within a few miles of each other. Having bailed out and survived, Jozef Jeka went on to continue with his career in the RAF.

The Search

With Jeka, Wick, and almost all other combatants from that day now deceased, and even eyewitnesses getting scarcer, one might think that the incident would be confined to museum or archive records, and that basically that would be that. But fortunately Britain has many aviation archaeological organisations who dedicate their time to the excavation and conservation of air-crash-related artefacts as well as keeping alive the memory of such

people, times, and events. For many years since the early 1980s quite a few organisations had looked for the impact point of Jeka's Hurricane, but none could locate it. Eyewitnesses stated that it had hit the ground vertically and 'disappeared'. Unfortunately, not one could pinpoint exactly where. So the classification 'disappeared' in relation to the Hurricane of Jozef Jeka seemed certain to remain as part of local folklore. However, to Gareth Jones, aviation archaeologist, and his colleagues, 'finding Jeka's Hurricane' was a challenge that could not be ignored. In total they made nine trips with eight metal detectorists to the alleged crash site; by the end of the eighth search all they had were six tiny crumpled and corroded pieces of metal. One more trip was planned to search the area where these had been located with a Forster model deep-seeking

detector. In one area a reading was obtained indicating that something of a metallic nature was deeply buried.

So, with this information and all the necessary permissions from landowners and a licence from the Ministry of Defence pursuant to the Protection of Military Remains Act 1986, a date was schedule to excavate the site in 2006. As soon as the top soil had been removed, traces of blue powdery aluminium oxide referred to by aviation archaeologists as 'Daz' become clearly evident in the soil. Then, as they continued to excavate, further fragments and 'Daz' ceased to appear – but the Forster still indicated that something remained buried much deeper. Excavating down to 10 feet, the digger bucket hit a firmly embedded large object.

This was carefully uncovered and seen to be a rotor hub or boss. This was more like it. The area was checked, and it was clear that something was still buried further down. However, a layer of backfill created a 3-foot area that was again totally devoid of finds. Further down in the sandy clay, more artefacts were once again evident: larger sections of compressed airframe were clearly seen and the surrounding soil was stained with oil and carbon deposits. At a depth of 20 feet it was now evident that the entire impacted front section of Hurricane V7535 still remained. For, lying at the bottom of the excavation was a mass of wreckage. The shattered Rolls Royce Merlin engine parts were seen to be in superb condition, as were the associated airframe and other artefacts.

Punching down through 20 feet of sand and clay, the wreckage had finally stopped on a layer of glacial gravel.

This page, clockwise:
The recovered Rolls-Royce Merlin engine; the control column after cleaning; manufacturer's instruction plate; detail of Rolls-Royce wording on engine rocker-cover.

ALL AIRCRAFT RECOVERY IMAGES BY GARETH JONES AND ASSOCIATES

This was an aviation archaeologist's dream; a large section of World War Two fighter aircraft bathed in oil and fuel, buried at depth. Everyone assumed that the state of preservation would be incredible, and they were right! As the cockpit area was unearthed, being carefully dug by hand-instruments, armour plate, and the radio as well as manufacturers labels and the Ki Gas primer were all recovered.

The anticipation was high, as part of the 'dream' is to uncover the control column or 'stick', as it is often referred to. Everything else seemed to be here. Then, from a pool of dark oil-saturated water came a length of tubular structure and chains and then with a suction noise the entire control column could be seen. Gareth carefully picked it up, the first person to hold the item since Josef Jeka

had done so some sixty-six years before!

Slightly to the side of this superb find were some large sections of folded paper, which, even though dirty, were clearly parts of flight maps.

The main undercarriage tyres could be seen in the mass of wreckage and, although damaged, were also in good stable condition. Another remarkable find was the 'Hawker Aircraft' main manufacturer's plate, which confirmed the precise identity of this Hurricane as that of the seat of Sergeant Jozef Jeka. The Merlin engine, somewhat worse for wear and dripping with oil and liquefied clay, was then lifted from its deep, dark, and oily grave and experienced daylight for the first time in nearly seven decades. Despite being shattered, the condition of its components was absolutely superb. The excavation was

This page, clockwise: Gunsight; Ki Gas primer; detail of Hawker Aircraft manufacturing plate; fragment of flying map.

'bottomed out' to check out whether any artefacts had penetrated further into the clay, but they had not. To ensure nothing was missed, the excavation was enlarged outwards, but again the soil was clear apart from a few perfectly preserved bullets.

As the members of the team sat down to examine the filthy creaking pile of metal that had once been a Hawker Hurricane fighter, it was clearly evident from their facial expressions that this was a highly successful dig. In fact, as digs go, this was pretty much an epic recovery and surely must rate extremely highly in the top 10 per cent of UK aircraft excavations both in quantity and, most importantly, in quality of recovered finds. One vital component of most such recoveries is the technical advance of metal detection equipment in the last four decades. Whether

you have a simple detector costing a £100, or sophisticated equipment costing thousands, the ability to achieve such astounding results cannot be ignored. One wonders if any local metal-detectorists may have found examples of fired MG17 or 20mm cannon shell casings that relate to this event – perhaps even examples that may have been fired by Major Helmut Wick himself.

Although there are a few flying examples of Hurricanes around the world, it is the dedication of people like Gareth Jones and his team that ensures examples of those aircraft that did not survive are recovered, conserved, and preserved. These relics continue, like their flying counterparts, to serve as memorials, in this case to all those brave young men who fought, survived, or perished in the skies over southern England in 1940. ∎

Crash Survivor

On 30 January 1942 Flight Lieutenant Czeslaw Kujawa, of the Polish Air Force, lifted his Wellington IC from the runway at RAF Bramcote, Warwickshire, England, heading north to carry out a cross-country training exercise. Sergeant Joseph Fusniak, the rear gunner in the all-Polish crew of six, sat in his turret, gazing out as the weather deteriorated, cloud thickened, and snow rushed past. Joseph would be the only survivor when the No. 18 Operational Training Unit Wellington bomber flew straight into the side of a hill.

Top: High above the village of Buckden in Wharfedale, Yorkshire, England a memorial stands to those who lost their lives when a Wellington bomber crashed on Buckden Pike in January 1942. Is that a fox head in the clouds?

CHAPTER EIGHT

Right: Polish air gunner Joseph Fusniak.

JOSEPH FUSNIAK

Joseph (or Jozef) Fusniak was born in Warsaw, Poland, on 10 May 1922, the son of a highly decorated soldier of World War One, who used his influence to provide Joseph with the opportunity to take the examination for entry to military school, which he passed. In 1938 Joseph took up elementary training with the Polish Air Force, learning the art of flying on gliders at Ustianowej in the Bieszczady Mountains, and then on RWD-8 trainer aircraft at Moderówce near Krosno, in the south-east of Poland. Eventually the threat of war with Germany became a reality. Joseph recalls, 'We were bombed, the whole airfield, all the planes were shot up and we were evacuated by train. Then in the middle of September the Russians came in.' At the Romanian border, 'there were masses and masses of people', and Joe and his colleagues were forced to give up any guns and ammunition prior to transfer to a camp at Slatina.

Our CO, at the border, took photographs of all of us, which he took to the Polish Embassy in Bucharest, where they could make civilian identity cards. While we were in Slatina camp, we had to escape one by one — the camp was a few hundred yards from the rail station. The

Romanian soldiers were absolutely terrible. Lots of them didn't have any shoes, and the officers used to bash them across the face with their hands — terrible. As they were guarding us, we used to say, 'Oh, that's a lovely gun. How does it work?' They would dismantle the gun to show us, meanwhile someone was under the wire and off they went. That's how I got away.

Joe removed all the buttons that could identify him as a member of the Polish Air Force and found a train bound for Bucharest. On arrival he was taken to the Polish Embassy, given civilian clothing and a false identity card, which had already been prepared. From Bucharest, Joe travelled by train to the Black Sea port of Balchik, where he managed to get on board a ship, with other Polish airmen, eventually arriving in Malta, 'where we were issued with white soft bread and cigarettes by the British'. From Malta Joe, on board the RMS *Franconia*, was taken to Marseilles, arriving on 12 November and from there to Lyons, 'the new HQ of the Polish Air Force, where we had to be sworn into the French Air Force'. Although Joe had been training for pilot duties, those who were already qualified received priority for training on French aircraft and postings to operational units. Frustration set in. 'Meantime a British officer came visiting and asked who would like to come and defend Britain. We had got so fed up waiting to be trained, so some of us volunteered.' Late in February 1940 Joe arrived at Southampton and proceeded to Eastchurch, where he was sworn into the Royal Air Force. Uniforms were issued, and he was transferred to Manston to await further training. But after 'doing nothing', he was sent to Blackpool, being used as a depot for Polish aircrew, prior to posting for further training or to operational units. Joe eventually did receive further basic pilot training, but a bout of flu interrupted his progression, and, again frustratingly, he was sent back to Blackpool. 'I was fed up waiting and they were short of air gunners, so I decided to go for that. I felt I had no option and was allocated to an air gunnery course at No. 18 Operational Training Unit at RAF Bramcote.'

Wallop!

At the end of his initial gunnery training, Joe was allocated to a crew, all Polish, and was told that he was going to be the rear gunner. 'There was a division between officers and NCOs; each kept to themselves in the Officers' Mess and the Sergeants' Mess. I knew the sergeants. During the flying you did your duty, there was no cohesion of brotherhood. That bond really came when you were operational flying over Germany.' But, prior to operations against the enemy, the crew had to carry out further training to hone their skills flying as part of a bomber crew unit. On 30 January 1942, Joe's crew was tasked with carrying out a training exercise in their Wellington IC.

The crew of Wellington IC N2848

Pilot:	Flight Lieutenant Czeslaw Kujawa
2nd pilot:	Pilot Officer Jerzy Polczyk
Observer:	Flight Officer Tadeusz Bieganski
Wireless Operator:	Sergeant Jan Sadowski
Front Gunner:	Sergeant John Tokarzewski
Rear Gunner:	Sergeant Joseph Fusniak

It was a very cold day and as I went to the Sergeants' Mess on my bicycle I walloped into someone and was bruised. I had my breakfast but didn't go to the crew briefing. I just put my flying jacket on and went to the plane. In the aircraft I didn't hear anything from the pilot. He didn't check if I was there or not.

The take-off was uneventful and course was set, but the weather deteriorated, 'then the snowflakes began to fall'. Joe looked on as the snowstorm grew in strength. He managed to get a glimpse of a railway line and station, which he reported to his pilot, who was 'at the time, I think, trying to get a fix. We were very low. After a while we went very straight and then WALLOP! Everything turned upside down, and I hit my head on a screw in the turret. Then it was very quiet. I put my hand behind my back, let the latch off and fell right out into the snow. There was terrible pain in my leg.' Joe gazed out into the blizzard. 'There was no plane, nothing. Just the wind blowing. I realised we had crashed, but there was no plane! I couldn't see a thing.' Then Joe heard moaning, 'sort of like a cow'.

I tried to walk but couldn't because of the pain, so I crawled towards the sound. I came across the skeleton of the plane, no engine, no wings, just a tube. I could still hear this moan, so I crawled a little bit further, and there were four people lying down, blown out of the aircraft from the impact. I could see their faces, all pale, not breathing. But I could still hear the voice. I thought, 'where's the cow?' I crawled a little bit further and then

I could see Jan, the radio operator. He was face down in the snow in a pool of blood, and I turned him over. I remembered there was a first-aid kit in the plane and I said, 'look, I'll crawl in and get you the first-aid kit'.

Joe dragged himself to the tattered fuselage. 'I couldn't find anything except two tins of tomato soup, a parachute and a strut.'

I crawled back, opened up the parachute and covered Jan. I told him, 'Look, I'll go and try to find some people.' I left him a tomato soup – how could he have opened a tin of soup? I went back to the rest of the crew. They were definitely dead. I started crawling with the wind, not against it. I didn't know where I was. All I knew was that we had been flying north. I didn't know that then, but I was going down the wrong side of the mountain. Something made me stop and think it was wrong, and, as I was crawling back to the plane, I saw paw prints. I thought it must be a fox and decided to follow it.

Fox Tracks

Joe came across a broken wall: 'It wasn't steep because of the snow and the fox had gone over.' Joe continued to follow the fox tracks, which suddenly turned to the right, thereby avoiding a precipice. The trail continued down, 'and I was following, crawling'.

I couldn't possibly walk. The snow was falling in my face and I was sweating with exertion. I said, 'Oh hell, where am I going', but I was going down. As I went further down, the snow started subsiding, but suddenly all the footmarks disappeared. I kept going in the same direction

"I tried to walk but couldn't because of the pain, so I crawled towards the sound. I came across the skeleton of the plane, no engine, no wings, just a tube."

and came to a wall. I was so exhausted; stars were coming into my eyes. I didn't know what to do. I thought I would go into the corner of the wall and rest there. I was just closing my eyes when a thought came into my mind not to go to sleep because I would freeze.

The sweat was starting to get cold, as was I. I had to move. Some instinct tells you to go on. The story that when you die your life goes before you — it's absolutely true. All my life: when I was young, school, training, France, Britain — flashes of pictures. When I opened my eyes, I could see a shaft of light passing over and at the bottom were dark patches. Perhaps they might be trees or a farm, or something. So I crawled over the top of the wall and it became much steeper. I was sliding and shouting 'help!'

His cry for help was heard. Below, Nannie Parker, daughter of William, the landlord of the White Lion Inn in the village of Cray, could hear something, but she thought it was a shepherd. She went and told her father, who came to listen, and Joe was seen. The exhausted airman collapsed, but the Parkers ran to his aid and dragged him into the pub. Initially, because of his faltering speech they believed he was German. 'They didn't know who I was. I was telling them, as I pointed up, that there were friends of mine — go and get them. When they took off my jacket they found out I was RAF and not German. I was given a stiff drink and they opened up the tomato soup. It was really hot, really nice.' As soon as the Parkers realised there were other airmen on the mountain, the alarm was raised. But the snowstorm prevented various attempts at a rescue until

Right: The fox head at the base of the Buckden Pike memorial.

STEVE DARLOW

URING THE WAR, Nottinghamshire, England, was the home for numerous RAF stations, from which many Polish airmen flew. At Newark-on-Trent an area was set aside for the burial of the men of the Polish Air Force who lost their lives. In total 397 Polish burials were carried out at the cemetery, including the colleagues of Joseph Fusniak, killed on Buckden Pike on 30 January 1942. **(For further cemetery details, see www.cwgc.org.)**

the following day, by which time it was too late. Joe would be the sole survivor from the crash.

Meantime, once the roads had been snow-ploughed, Joe was taken to Skipton to receive medical treatment, and his leg was encased in plaster. Eventually Joe would return to RAF Bramcote but was sent to Scotland to recuperate. After a few weeks he returned once more to Bramcote to join another crew. 'I went right through training with them. I still wanted to fly. I was keen to fight the Germans.' He would, and once more he would confront death. The second part of Joe's story will feature in a future volume of *Fighting High – World War Two – Air Battle Europe*. ∎

2nd pilot:
Pilot Officer J. Polczyk

Wireless Operator:
Sergeant J. Sadowski

Front Gunner:
Sergeant J. A. Tokarzewski

Pilot: Flight Lieutenant
C. Kujawa

Observer: Flight Officer
T. J. Bieganski

Polish Memorial,
Newark-on-Trent

Left: In recognition of his attempt to save the life of wireless operator Jan Sadowski, Joseph Fusniak received the British Empire Medal from RAF Bomber Command's Commander-in-Chief Sir Arthur Harris at RAF Bramcote in May 1942.

Left: After the war Joseph Fusniak often visited the site of the fateful crash and during 1973, with the help of some locals, he set about building the memorial cross on Buckden Pike. Embedded into the base are fragments of the wrecked Wellington. Regular remembrance services are still held at the memorial.

A Journey into

The spring, summer, and autumn months of 1943 saw an escalation in the Allied bomber offensive against Germany. The Royal Air Force's Bomber Command threw all its weight into the Battle of the Ruhr, a sustained campaign attacking the industrial heartland of Germany. Bomber Command airmen, in response, had to confront the escalation in their enemy's night aerial and ground defences. The damage to the Ruhr industry and cities was extensive, achieved at a considerable cost in machines and airmen to Bomber Command. One British airman who fought and survived these night battles was flight engineer Nathan 'Nat' Bury, who earned the Distinguished Flying Medal 'in recognition of gallantry and devotion to duty in the execution of air operations'. In recent years, Nat recorded his 'few thoughts and ramblings on service life'.

the Unknown

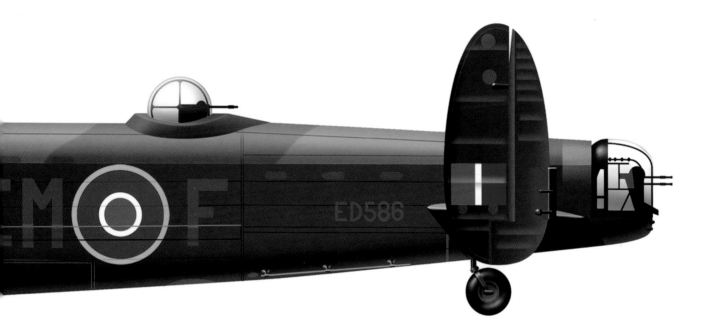

In February 1943 Nat Bury arrived at No. 1654 Heavy Conversion Unit, RAF Wigsley, to team up with his future operational bomber crew.

What can one say about crewing up? Only the RAF could devise such a method. Basically you were on your own mate, left to your own devices. We engineers and an equal number of mid-upper gunners were dumped in a hangar and told, 'find yourself a crew and get on with it'. The pilot, navigator, bomb aimer, wireless operator/air gunner, and rear gunner had already been in this situation at an operational training unit, having crewed up in similar circumstances, and already had quite a number of hours together as a crew. On the other hand, the flight engineers (especially in the early days before the direct-entry scheme came in), having served on operational stations either as engine or airframe fitters, imagined, quite incorrectly of course, that they could pick out the best crews. This was wishful thinking on our part, but probably, because of this seemingly haphazard system, most crews got along amazingly well and very quickly gelled as a team. I can't recall whether, with my own crew, I found them or they sorted me out, but be that as it may, after well over fifty years, all seven of us were still in contact and on speaking terms. Even after sixty-five years (having lost 'Mac', our rear gunner, in 1996, Jimmy, our navigator, and Ken, our bomb aimer), four members, all octogenarians, are in regular contact. Perhaps the RAF knew something other air forces were unaware of when it came to crewing up.*

I suppose the biggest shock on arrival at *Wigsley* was seeing *Avro Manchester* aircraft at dispersal. We were already aware of their reputation for being under-powered. However, up to this period, the flight engineers had very little or no flying experience and were therefore

finally the runway light up. Bloody marvellous.

In March 1943, when we arrived at No. 207 Squadron, RAF Langar, Nottinghamshire, crews were in extremely short supply, and replacements were warmly welcomed. The idea was to replace lost crews quickly and

> "We did not find out until much later, thank goodness, that some of the older hands looked upon our new crew as a motley bunch and estimated we would probably get the chop by the sixth operation."

keen to get some in and sample the delights of flying, even on Manchesters (idiots). After about a week, we happily transferred to the reliable Lancaster.

Of all the training undertaken so far, this was certainly the most exciting; the first time I had ever flown. Even the gunnery course had been carried out on the ground. The experience of a few circuits and bumps, as they were termed with an instructor, followed by actually being part of a crew, was overwhelming. To commence with I was nervous and a little apprehensive but none the less excited. The first long cross-country exercise was, along with my first night flight, a wonderful, not-to-be-forgotten, experience. At night, to see the perimeter, followed by the funnel, the angle of glide indicator and

for huts not to be left empty. It wasn't easy getting to know other crews who were coming and going in rapid succession. It could be demoralising for those remaining, so the name of the game was not to leave too many gaps and vacant places, especially in the messes at meal times. As long as there were a sufficient number of bodies milling around, everything appeared normal, and nobody seemed to worry. We did not find out until much later, thank goodness, that some of the older hands looked upon our new crew as a motley bunch and estimated we would probably get the chop by the sixth operation. Bloody decent lot of so and sos. I am happy and delighted to have eventually proved them wrong.

During the early part of our tour we were unfortunate

Right: Flight Engineer's course (No. 7) at RAF St Athan, November 1942. Nat is seated second from the right.

The 'Motley Crew' – the lowest of the low, an all-sergeant crew, the minimum rank for aircrew.

Clockwise from left: Flight Engineer: Sergeant Nathan Bury, 'Blondie' from Lancashire; Pilot: Sergeant Jack Stephens, 'Steve' from Devon; Navigator: Sergeant James Love, 'Jimmy' or 'Jim' from Canada; Bomb Aimer: Sergeant Kenneth Bate, 'Bate' or 'Ken' from the West Midlands; Wireless Operator/ Air Gunner: Sergeant Jack Pegrum, 'Lucky' from Essex; Rear Gunner: Sergeant Arthur McDavitt, 'Mac' from Surrey; Mid-Upper Gunner: Sergeant Arthur Barfoot, 'Joe' from Dorset.

Imagine the range of accents to be heard over the aircraft intercom system. Although it was necessary to announce who was speaking when talking through this system (navigator to skipper, rear gunner to skipper, etc.), we recognised immediately from our accents who was on the other end.

to experience two abortive sorties, commonly known as DNCOs (Duty Not Carried Out). The first DNCO occurred on our second trip, which was termed 'Gardening', the service jargon for mine laying, in the Bay of Biscay. Quite sometime after take-off we lost power on one engine, which had to be shut down and feathered (stopping the propeller rotating). We decided to carry on until, two hours into the flight, another engine started to lose power and overheat. This put paid to any thought of completing this particular type of operation. To continue on a mission where mines have to be laid from a relatively low altitude and with such reduced power would have been completely stupid, if not suicidal. Although we were still wet behind the ears, we were not complete idiots.

The second DNCO happened on our fifth trip, to Frankfurt. *Again*, just two hours into the operation our compasses packed up, completely haywire. Once more prudence won the day, and we returned. We were learning quickly. Oddly enough, these two abortive sorties were in the same aircraft and fortunately for us were the only two throughout our tour.

I suppose that, in comparison to many crews, we had a reasonably good tour. Although every operation had its moments of anxiety, only six of them gave us serious cause for concern. These were as follows.

One Hell of a Long Way

16 April 1943: our eighth operation and the first of two

to Pilsen, which is one hell of a long way over enemy territory. In the target area we were picked up on radar, monitored and subjected to a very intensive barrage of fire from enemy ack ack batteries, subsequently receiving several hits, causing quite a bit of damage, which

Right and opposite page: Two of Nat's collection of raid mementoes issued by No. 5 Group in recognition of specific raids.

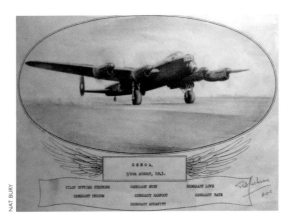

NAT BURY

GENOA,
7/8th AUGUST, 1943.

fortunately turned out to be only superficial. There were not any casualties and the aircraft plodded on regardless. On our return we were diverted to Tangmere, West Sussex. Although we were badly holed by the flak, it did not prevent us from making a one-hour return flight back to base the next day, making this a round trip of nine hours and twenty-five minutes, and sadly the total losses on that particular operation were quite high. Four weeks later we were ordered once again to Pilsen. Naturally we did not exactly relish the thought of a return trip. Once bitten, twice shy. However, all went well, a fairly comfortable operation without incident.

One Hell of a Fright

14 June 1943: the seventeenth operation and this time to Oberhausen. We were well and truly coned, caught by a large battery of powerful searchlights, of which one was a master beam that monitored and locked on to us. It appeared the Krauts were throwing everything under the sun up at us. It took us ages to shrug them off, during which time I thrust the throttles through what was referred to as the 'gate' to boost plus twelve, in order to produce full power; the maximum we were permitted and then only for a period of five minutes unless you wished to tear the engines from their bearings. During this power surge we lost several thousands of feet in height. My lasting recollection of this incident were the extraordinary 'G' forces as we pulled out of our dive. My feet were firmly anchored to the floor of the aircraft as

if held down by lead weights, and the navigator went berserk when his charts and equipment started to leave his table and float merrily away during our diving tactics. Even our heavy parachutes were no match against such forces. Frankly, one hell of a fright.

Almighty Crash

5 July 1943: operation number twenty and the first of two to Cologne. We were just commencing our bombing run into the target area, when all of sudden there was a resounding almighty crash and the aircraft almost turned on its back. How the skipper kept control and brought us back to some form of normality amazed us; it required a show of brute force and strong nerve. I seem to remember, at the skipper's request, urgently spinning the trimming tab at a hell of a rate of knots, and somehow or other we were once more the right way up, on an even keel, still in the air and flying. Whatever damage we had sustained did not appear to have rendered us helpless, the engines were throbbing beautifully, height was being maintained, and we did not seem to be losing any fuel. Restarting our bomb run, we released our load, and before completing our run managed to take a photograph of the actual aiming point. For this photograph each of the crew received a memento signed by the Air Officer Commanding No. 5 Group. On return to base we discovered the starboard aileron had been almost completely torn away; the good old faithful Lancaster could certainly stand a tremendous amount of punishment. In due course it was established that a 30lb incendiary bomb from another aircraft had hit us fair and square; miraculously it had missed the main fuel tanks and pipelines. God only knows what might have happened had it been his 4,000lb high-explosive 'cookie', as it was termed. Three nights later we were over Cologne again and, as with the previous Pilsen trip, not very happy to return to the same target after such a scare.

One amusing follow-up to the 'Cologne' incident was that, in spite of A.V. Roe having a major repair depot on the airfield, it was necessary for a replacement aileron to be ordered and brought from another RAF airfield, Bottesford, a few miles away. This duly arrived and was gently placed on the ground close to the aircraft at dispersal, ready for fitting. However, before it could be assembled, the truck that had delivered it accomplished a perfect demolition job by reversing over it, which naturally required a return journey to Bottesford for a further replacement. Suffice it to say, this incident did not amuse the hierarchy.

One of the Great Raids

17 August 1943: our twenty-seventh operation, as we were clocking them up and approaching the end of our tour of operations, was to Peenemünde, the German experimental rocket research establishment. It was one of the great raids of World War Two. There were two main problems: first, the mission had to be carried out in brilliant moonlight; secondly, in order to have any chance of success on such a difficult target, we were required to drop our 'cookies' from the minimum height of about 6,000 feet, not the normal 18,000–20,000 feet. It was a seven-hour flight to be carried out by three waves of aircraft. The first wave got away extremely lightly. The second wave did suffer but not too badly. By the time the third and last wave arrived, the German night fighters, which at first had been misled by a spoof raid to Berlin, had finally got their act together and in brilliant moonlight (as bright as day) were waiting for us. All hell broke loose, with aircraft appearing to go down left, right, and centre. To make matters more daunting, No. 5 Group, ours, had been briefed and ordered to make what was called a time and distance run on the final leg into the target area before releasing our lethal cargo. This required finding a particular but easily identifiable prominent landmark a few miles from the target before

SPEZIA
18/19 4 43

SGT STEPHENS, SGT BURY, SGT LOVE,
SGT PEGRUM, SGT BARFOOT, SGT McDAVITT,
SGT LLEWELLYN

NAT BURY

flying straight and level on a particular heading, at a certain speed and height for a given time before releasing the bomb load. Flying straight and level in the vicinity of the target area was not considered the healthiest of pastimes. Our Canadian navigator, not being renowned for his politeness or choice of vocabulary, wrote in his flight log, 'there must be hundreds of the buggers',

meaning the fighters. This was maybe a little exaggerated, but he was often in trouble over various words of wisdom when making up his flight logs. It was witnessing so many aircraft going down in flames that made this particular raid so scary and outstanding in my memory. As far as I can remember, it was the first and only time our navigator came from behind his blackout curtain, said a few choice words, then disappeared back behind his curtain.

This operation was followed a few nights later with a seven-and-a-quarter-hour jaunt to Berlin, which was surprisingly quite uneventful, at least for our crew.

Prang Number One

It had to happen sooner or later. This occurred on 20 September 1943, surprisingly returning not from an operational flight but from a night bombing exercise. After successfully completing the exercise, we arrived back and orbited base, requesting and being given permission to land, but then the airfield perimeter and funnel lights, which were meant to assist landing, failed to appear. After many pleadings with control to switch them on and being repeatedly told they were on, which they were not, we had no alternative but to land without them. Unfortunately we overshot the runway and crashed into the perimeter boundary, causing considerable damage to the aircraft but, amazingly, no harm to ourselves. As we came to a stop, a female voice from air control came over the communication system and asked if the funnel was off, and we, being somewhat annoyed and shaken, replied that yes the funnel was off and we were off the effing runway. I admit this was not very polite but under the circumstances was somewhat understandable. Typical of the RAF, the following day we received a thorough dressing-down from the CO for our bad language, which had been heard by a few WAAFs in the control tower; nothing was said about the kite. It appears that the control tower replica of the airfield was nicely lit up, but not the main lights.

Under Attack

22 September 1943: Two more missions to go… and we were engaged by a Me110. Fortunately for us, he was either a rotten shot or very scared of the return fire from both our rear and mid-upper gunners. Consequently, after a couple of passes, he cleared off. It was probably a novice or a pilot running short of fuel or ammunition.

```
Combat Report Excerpt:
Night: 22/23 September 1943
Squadron: 207
Captain F/O Stephens
Station: Langar
A/C Letter: 'B'

On the night of 22/23rd September,
1943, Lancaster 'B' of No. 207 Squadron
was detailed to attack Hanover at 21.34
hours where, in the target area, flying
at 14,000 feet at an I.A.S. of 170
m.p.h. a Me.110, with day camouflage,
was seen at 500 yards dead astern and
slightly down. The enemy aircraft
followed the Lancaster as if to attack
but the Rear Gunner opened fire at 500
yards as standard corkscrew action was
taken. The enemy aircraft did not open
fire and dived away, down, when at 400
yards range.

No claims are made.

At the time of the attack visibility
was very clear and very bright
conditions prevailed.

MONICA gave the first and constant
indication of the presence of the
fighter

Number of rounds fired: 200 approx.

Rear Gunner: Sgt MCDAVITT. No. 1
A.A.S. and No. 16 O.T.U.
```

23 September 1943: on our final operation of the tour we sallied forth to Mannheim without too many problems, but on the return journey we were once again attacked by a Me110. This time, however, we were out of luck, for the port outer engine burst into flames. I immediately shut it down, cut off the fuel supply and feathered the propeller; bang went my finger on the fire extinguisher button, I prayed like hell and, fortunately, after what seemed like hours, the fire slowly died down. Evidently lady luck had quickly returned and was still with us. The grinning old reaper wasn't yet ready and waiting. Being on the last operation of a tour is no picnic; nerves are more edgy than normal, as you wonder whether your luck will hold for a few more hours, and there are a host of different scenarios going through your mind. However, having shut down this particular engine and used the fire extinguisher, we were left with a problem.

With one engine out of action, a Lancaster, once trimmed, will continue to cruise along quite merrily. However, on multi-engine aircraft, each engine drives a number of ancillary components, such as alternators, hydraulic pumps, and compressors. These, in turn, operate a variety of systems without which (apart from some emergency procedures using compressed air stored in bottles, of which some can be used only once and for which manual operation is extremely slow) such things as interior heating, under-carriage operation, some navigational equipment, flaps control, turret rotation, and machine-gun firing mechanisms would be useless. Bearing this in mind and still being harassed by this Me110, and also because of the particular ancillary components our dud engine would normally drive, we had two choices: either leave well alone with our rear turret out of action and pray like hell, or unfeather whenever requested by the rear gunner. This allows the engine components to turn over. However, when this happens, although there is no power (just the reverse), there is quite a drag, but at least the propeller rotates at the same revolutions as the good engines and the ancillaries work almost as normal. Unfortunately, if you choose this method, there may be a heavy price to pay; there is a possibility that the engine may reignite, and, having used the fire extinguisher, you could be in serious trouble. It is also detrimental to the engine, which is almost certain to seize up completely, losing all its components for the remainder of the operation. You pays your money, you takes your choice. We figured the lesser of the two evils was to unfeather whenever required on instructions from our rear gunner, and fortunately we got away with it. It was bad luck on the engine though. All these decisions have to be taken within seconds, with no opportunity for hanging about.

During our final debriefing after landing, we explained the course of action we had taken, which, in any case, was registered in both the navigator's and my own flight engineer's logs. The engineer's log had to be written up every twenty minutes for some aspects of engine control and every hour for other systems, apart from recording unusual incidents and of course keeping a record of the fuel consumption. What the squadron ground engineer officer said to me after the engine had been examined is not repeatable. Fortunately the CO came to my assistance with a few choice words of his own about what action you are able to take in a crisis, thereby ending our first tour of operations.

The raid to Mannheim on 23 September 1943 brought Nat's first tour to a close. Shortly after he was awarded the Distinguished Flying Medal, the citation recording 'Flight Sgt. Bury, as Flight Engineer, has participated in successful attacks upon Essen, Kiel and Berlin and many distant targets such as Spezia, Pilsen and Peenemünde.' In September 1943 the citation stated, 'one engine of his aircraft caught fire while over the target, and immediately afterwards the bomber was attacked by an enemy fighter. This airman at once extinguished the fire which enabled his captain and gunners to concentrate on the combat. Flight Sgt. Bury's devotion to duty during long flights has inspired confidence in other members of his crew and contributed to the successful completion of many sorties.'

Happy Days
On looking back at his tour of operations, especially when he was off duty, or when operations were scrubbed, Nat recalls RAF Langar as a very happy station.

It was particularly so because it was a one-squadron-only station, which eliminated any rivalry that might have occurred. Being there in the spring and summer, we had the best of the weather, which contributed to the speed at which we completed our stint. Each crew had its own Nissen hut, which was rather basic but none the less cosy. Being some distance from the airfield and flight officer, we each acquired a rather rickety battered sit up and beg bicycle, which enabled us to travel to and fro. The local villages and watering holes we frequented were also some distance from our accommodation and messes. Our favourite watering hole was a delightful old pub called The Plough situated in the village of Stathern about 3 miles away; therefore our crude form of transport served us well whenever we found time to pay it a visit. However, God help any other road users who got in our way during our somewhat unsteady weaving and precarious journey back to base late at night in the blackout when we were fully tanked up. During this trip we often called in at the flight offices and locker rooms in order to inhale a few whiffs of pure oxygen at the oxygen mask test beds. This had the amazing, but very temporary, effect of

sobering us up before we carried on to the billets and turned in for the night.

One great asset to the area was a nearby hostel housing a large number of Land Army girls, I believe about forty. Our bomb aimer eventually married one of them. The girls were jolly good company and a wonderful source of extra rations, such as eggs, cheese, apples, pears, and milk from the local farms on which they were employed. One farm adjoining the airfield dispensed delicious sandwiches of hard boiled eggs, cheese or ham, at a few pence a throw. With the tragic loss of many crews and so few successfully completing a tour of operations, we got to know some of the girls very well. Indeed, one of the Land Army girls wrote a song about the crew as we finished

"We did meet up again forty-six years later, and have remained in touch ever since."

our tour. The Land Army girls, along with the station's WAAFs, girls from the local ack-ack sites, and the locals themselves, were most welcome at all the village dances and functions. As for Sergeants' Mess parties, they, from time to time and for no apparent reason, tended to erupt into mayhem. The least said the better. They were certainly not meant for the faint-hearted, and navigating back to our bunks afterwards was a nightmare. Happy days!

Prior to Nat's crew's next posting, they had their end-of-tour party with their ground crew, and then some leave, with the 'thought of not returning to play games and dice with the old reaper for a few months, but with the sadness of not knowing if we would ever meet up with each other in the future'. As it was, each of the crew went his separate way. Nat went on to carry out numerous instructional duties with Bomber Command and at one time was posted overseas to serve with No. 45 Group, Atlantic Transport Command.

We did meet up again forty-six years later, and have remained in touch ever since. Eventually we ended the war with Steve, Jimmy and myself as Flight Lieutenants, Joe as a Flying Officer and Ken, Lucky and Mac as Warrant Officers. Steve and Jimmy had been awarded the DFC, Ken, Lucky, Mac, Joe and yours truly had been awarded the DFM, but most importantly we were in one piece. Not too bad for what began as a motley old bunch. ■

On 20 December 1943 1st Lieutenant Waldo Crosson lifted his Eighth Air Force 381st Bomb Group B-17 Flying Fortress from the runway at Ridgewell, Essex, England, at the start of a mission to attack the docks and submarine pens at Bremen. Waldo Crosson and his crew would not be returning. Just over fifty-seven years after the fateful flight, Allen Crosson would visit Germany and meet the local people who witnessed the demise of his father's bomber.

Flying Fortress Down

Right: Crew picture taken at Dyersburg, Tennessee, in July 1943 during the third phase of B-17 transition training, just before Waldo Crosson's crew went overseas.

Standing left to right: Staff Sergeant Steve Bulsok – ball turret gunner; Staff Sergeant Robert Eloe – tail gunner; Staff Sergeant Jesse Glawson – right waist gunner; Technical Sergeant Robert McFarlane – radio operator; Staff Sergeant Norman Klima – left waist gunner; Technical Sergeant John Allen – engineer/ top turret gunner. Front left to right: 2nd Lieutenant John 'Andy' Curran – bombardier; 2nd Lieutenant Edward Burke – navigator; 2nd Lieutenant Waldo Crosson – pilot; 2nd Lieutenant Gayle Messenger – co-pilot.

ALLEN CROSSON

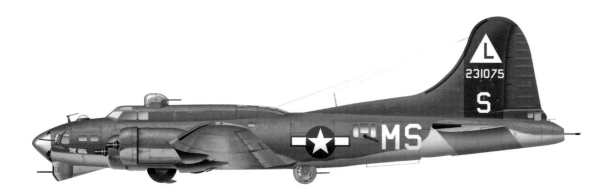

In the summer of 2001, the son of an Eighth Air Force airman made a trip to Germany. It was, as Allen Crosson recalls, 'a pilgrimage, some might say, to a quiet, rural place in the countryside north-west of Bremen; near the villages of Albstedt and Finna; a place where, on a December day in 1943, the life of my father, and the lives of nine other young American flyers, changed for ever'.

I stood on ground little changed over the past fifty-eight years, ground that held nightmarish memories for a German woman and man who were very young people in December 1943. And I listened to eyewitness descriptions of the final airborne moments of a B-17 Flying Fortress; and the death of a young American co-pilot seeking escape from a dying bomber.

Bail Out

Allen Crosson's journey of discovery had started two years previously, when he had responded to a question posed by a German man, on the Internet, concerning the bombing of a bridge near his home town in southern Germany, by American bombers, in the latter stages of World War Two. In response, Allen asked the man if he had any contacts in the north of Germany who could help him research a raid on Bremen in December 1943. 'In a matter of days this individual had contacted the mayor of Albstedt, Germany, and provided information regarding the specific details I had requested. Thus began a correspondence that culminated in the visit to Germany and the opportunity to experience something I had previously believed impossible.'

The event that led me to Germany, fifty-eight years after the fact, was the premature end to an Eighth Air Force raid against the docks and submarine pens at Bremen, some 25 kilometres inland from the North Sea, on the Weser River, and a high-priority target. The submarine

THE EIGHTH AIR Force despatched 546 bombers to Bremen on 20 December 1943. By the end of the day twenty-seven were recorded as Missing in Action. The war diary of the 535th Bomb Squadron (part of the 381st Bomb Group) recorded:

'Tinkertoy', possibly the best-known Fortress on the field, and widely publicized at home, was one of two squadron ships missing in action today, on a mission to Bremen. Lts Crosson and Lane, and their crews, are down on the group's toughest mission in many weeks, the heaviest loss since Dec 1. Reports say 'Tinkertoy' was rammed from behind by a German fighter, but no report on 'The Rebel' flown by Lt Crosson.

Strike photos show excellent bombing results for this group. Flak was the 105mm stuff, accurate and in large doses in the target area. The Nazi fighters shown no reluctance to come on in through it to get to the Forts. Some 40 or 50 checkered FW190s, flown by pilots our men described as 'plenty hot', offered stiff opposition. Also in the fight were Me109 and ME110 rocket throwers.

S/Sgts Phillipuk and Ford are each credited with one e/a destroyed. Sgt Charles D. Middleton was severely frostbitten and hospitalized; the Purple Heart is now being awarded for such cases. None of the gunners thinks too highly of the idea.

LIEUTENANT WALDO CROSSON'S B17 S/42-31075 – THE REBEL. ILLUSTRATION BY PETE WEST

Right: Waldo Crosson, Pecos, Texas, during basic flight training.

Inset: Jim Opitz, the co-pilot to Waldo Crosson on the Bremen mission. Jim had lost his original crew on 1 December 1943 over Leverkusen, Germany. He was then assigned to Crosson's crew to replace the original co-pilot, Gayle Messenger, who had a problem with his ears.

ALLEN CROSSON

**Missing in Action 535th Bomb Squadron
S/42-31075 – 'The Rebel'**

Crosson, Waldo B.	1st Lt	POW
Opitz, James R.	2nd Lt	KIA
Burke, Edward J.	2nd Lt	POW
Curran, John J.	2nd Lt	POW
Allen, John L.	T/Sgt	POW
McFarlane, Robert	S/Sgt	POW
Bulsok, Steve F.	S/Sgt	POW
Glawson, Jesse J.	S/Sgt	POW
Klima, Norman J.	S/Sgt	KIA
Eloe, Robert N.	S/Sgt	KIA

Today's mission would be the final one for Jim, as well as for gunners Robert Eloe and Norman Klima, this side of eternity.

The mission proceeded as briefed from take-off until the initial point (IP) of the bomb run. As the formation turned at the IP, vicious, concentrated fighter attacks began on the low group of the lead formation. Lieutenant Crosson's plane, 'The Rebel', was heavily hit by Me109 fighters and flak and began to trail behind the formation with an engine on fire and crewmen wounded. 'The Rebel' was kept under control with the auto-pilot, a factor that would affect the plane's eventual fate, and successfully bombed the target. After 'bombs away',

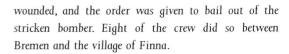

Lieutenant Crosson cut short the turn to the rally point and came back under the formation for about 30 seconds. 'The Rebel' was on fire, losing altitude and was still under attack by Me109 fighters. The formation course was to the north-west of Bremen, and soon the lives of some young German civilians would meld with those of Lieutenant Crosson's crew. Seven of 'The Rebel' crewmen were wounded, and the order was given to bail out of the stricken bomber. Eight of the crew did so between Bremen and the village of Finna.

After bailing out, Waldo Crosson was knocked unconscious and the waist gunner Jesse Glawson cracked an ankle bone, because of the frozen ground. Other crew members escaped relatively unscathed, with the exception of Jim Opitz, Norman Klima, and Robert Eloe. In 2001

pen stands today, just as it did in 1943, except that the structure is now abandoned, fenced in concrete, and inaccessible from the river – a haunting reminder of the fruits of slave labour and the dreams of a madman.

The raid of 20 December started out routinely, with formation assembly completed in the clear, cold, unlimited visibility skies over England. The co-pilot in Lieutenant Crosson's crew was 2nd Lieutenant Jim Opitz, a replacement who had lost his original crew in early December and who was taking over for the regular co-pilot, Gayle Messenger, who had trouble with his ears.

ALLEN CROSSON

Right: 'The Rebel'.

Waldo Crosson's son was able to reflect upon what had happened in his father's aircraft on the fateful day.

Standing in a misting rain, on a country road near Albstedt, Germany, I tried to picture in my mind the last moments of the cohesive bomber crew. The first fighter attack at the IP inflicted severe damage to the B-17 and some of the men were wounded. The bomber was on fire, none of the gunners was sure what was happening. Do they jump or stay with the plane?

Robert Eloe, tail gunner, was probably one of the first gunners to be wounded. The tail gun was one of the first gun positions to be silenced if a successful fighter attack was to be made on a Fortress. Eloe bailed out, only to die later on the ground. The waist, ball turret, and radio operator positions were hit badly in the second fighter attack after 'bombs away'. The left waist gunner, Norman Klima, was mortally wounded in a hail of 20mm cannon fire and fell against the ball turret. Robert McFarlane, radio operator, Steve Bulsok, ball turret gunner, and Jesse Glawson, right waist gunner, were all wounded but managed to escape the crippled bomber.

In the forward section of the plane, the officers and flight engineer were having their own problems. Both pilots were badly wounded, the cockpit was blasted by cannon and machine-gun fire and, as 'The Rebel' lagged behind the formation, the order was given to bail out. Lieutenant Crosson, who had been flying with the auto-pilot, set 'The Rebel' into a slightly nose down left-hand turn. This gave the crew a chance to get away from the plane as they bailed out.

The pilot, bombardier, navigator, and flight engineer managed to jump. Lieutenant Opitz, badly wounded, weak from loss of blood and in shock, probably passed out on the flight deck. With eight of the crew free of the ship, 'The Rebel' continued to descend in a left-hand turn, north-west of the target. At some point, two Me109 fighters picked up 'The Rebel' and continued to pursue it. Possibly thinking that the B-17 was still under control, even though two engines were by now on fire, the German pilots continued to make firing passes on the descending Fortress.

As the plane continued its auto-pilot-controlled descent, Jim Opitz finally regained consciousness on the floor of the flight deck. He must have realised that 'The Rebel' was very near the ground and knew that his only chance for survival was to get out of the plane. With some last reserve of strength he was able to attach his chest pack parachute and reach either the forward escape hatch or the open bomb bay. He fell free from the plane.

Witnesses

A Harry Ahrens, who was 14 years old at the time of the incident, lived, as he did in 2001, in the village of Finna, 12 miles north-west of Bremen. Herr Ahrens is the only living witness who saw Jim Opitz jump from 'The Rebel'. Allen Crosson relates what he saw.

Harry was standing near his home, about noon, on 20 December 1943 and heard the noise of aircraft engines approaching, from the direction of Bremen, at what seemed to be a very low altitude. Suddenly, through the trees, he saw an American Flying Fortress pursued by two Me109 fighters. Two of the bomber's engines were on fire, and the German fighters were shooting at the bomber. As the bomber passed the village, turning in the direction of Albstedt, Harry saw a man drop from the B-17 at an altitude of about 300–400 metres. The airman fell to earth about 300 metres from where Harry was standing.

Crashing through a line of trees, along a dirt road, the airman struck the frozen ground head first, his parachute never opening. Jim Opitz's valiant struggle for survival

Left: Harry Ahrens pointing in the air, at the spot where Jim Opitz came to earth.

ALLEN CROSSON

CHAPTER TEN

Clockwise from top:
Local German historian
Hans Kurth, left, with
Harry Ahrens, middle,
and Allen Crosson, near
the fire house in the
village of Finna. The
bodies of Norman
Klima and Jim Opitz
were taken to the fire
house in Finna on
21 December 1943
and placed there, with
the bodies of six other
airmen, until they could
be picked up and taken
to Bremerhaven for
burial.

The fire house at Finna.

July 2001. The original
Cordes farmhouse in
front of the barn, with
a crop of corn growing.
Waldo Crosson's B-17
crashed just out of the
picture to the right.

Photographs of the
wreckage of 'The Rebel'.

ALLEN CROSSON

FRAU CORDES, COURTESY OF ALLEN CROSSON

ALLEN CROSSON

ALLEN CROSSON

ended at the base of a tree, on a footpath, in the village of Finna, Germany. Harry ran to the airman's body and noted the bullet wounds in his chest, the head injuries from the fall and the airman's name on his flight jacket. He remembers the scene today, fifty-eight years later, as if it happened yesterday.

Jim's body was covered with his parachute, left where it had fallen, until the following day about noon. His body was then moved to the fire house in Finna, where it was picked up, about 4 p.m. on 21 December, and taken to the Garrison Cemetery, at Bremerhaven, for burial.

A further witness to the event, a 21-year-old German farm girl, was near her home outside the village of Albstedt when she heard aircraft engines.

She saw a B-17, then very close to the ground, just above the trees, circling down as if attempting to land in the corn field adjacent to the house. At least one Me109 was still shooting at the bomber, and the girl was very afraid

young woman went to see Norman's body and observed that he had been shot in the chest and side. Other than the bullet wounds, his body was unmarked by the explosion and she thought, 'He's only sleeping.' Norman's body was picked up about noon that day and taken to the fire house in Finna. Here it was placed with Jim Opitz's body, and the bodies of six other airmen, to be taken to Bremerhaven later that day for burial.

"As if by intent, the plane struck the ground almost in the centre of the corn field; about 50 metres from her house, and disintegrated in a massive fireball as the aviation fuel ignited."

that the Fortress was going to hit her home. As if by intent, the plane struck the ground almost in the centre of the corn field; about 50 metres from her house, and disintegrated in a massive fireball as the aviation fuel ignited. Pieces of the bomber flew in every direction, and one of the engines was thrown over a quarter of a mile distant. The fire burned for several hours, and exploding machine-gun ammunition and oxygen tanks forced the woman, and her mother, to abandon the farm, until the next day, in fear of their lives.

The next morning the woman returned to the field and took three photos of the wreckage, a very serious offence as the taking of pictures, or any contact with enemy soldiers, was forbidden. A section of the vertical stabiliser (minus the rudder and tail gunner compartment) and the right horizontal stabiliser with elevator, and the ball turret, were the only large pieces of wreckage in the field. Everything else was twisted and scattered debris.

Sometime that morning the body of Norman Klima was discovered, over 150 metres from the centre of the crash, thrown there by the force of the explosion. The

So the mission ended; and there were the quick and the dead. The survivors went to hospitals and prison camps; the young German civilians went about their lives in a war-torn country, burying the memories of what they had witnessed. However, those memories do not fade. Frau Cordes, the young German woman of long ago, today still living next to the cornfield, thinks of the exploding bomber, and the aftermath of the crash, every day. ∎

WITH GREAT REGRET

Les Gill, second from the left, takes a ride on the bomb load, at No. 460 Squadron. Australian 'Jack' Chadwick-Bates on the left, Arthur Rolfe, middle, Bill Raper, second from right, Clarence Gynther on the right.

On New Year's Day 1944, RAF Bomber Command stations were hives of activity as ground crew prepared their bombers for a raid that night and aircrew tested their aircraft and went through their pre-operational routines. That night 421 Lancasters would take off from English runways, heading east, with full bomb loads, intent on causing widespread destruction in the German 'Big City' – Berlin. The next day, against the names of twenty-eight Lancaster crews, 'Failed to Return' would be recorded in squadron record books. Four of these crews had been flying No. 156 Squadron Lancasters. In the turret of one was Flight Sergeant Dennis Mills DFM; the wireless operator in another was Warrant Officer Leslie Gill.

Right: Bomber Command Air Gunner Dennis Mills.

DAVID MILLS

Right: RAF apprentice Les Gill, 1939.

MICHAEL COLLINS

During the late autumn and winter months of 1943–4 Bomber Command airmen committed themselves to the 'Battle of Berlin'. The 'Big City' soon earned a reputation: a long flight over enemy territory and a well-defended target. As the losses mounted, crews that returned adopted a very insular approach, protecting themselves from the realities of what they were part of.

Flight Engineer Jack Watson DFM recalled the first time he saw Berlin under attack, 'burning like mad, a huge red glow in the sky, and that was from fifty miles away'. Jack flew on operations to Berlin four times while with No. 12 Squadron early in 1944. (In March 1944 he would take up duties with No. 156 Squadron.) 'It would take nearly forty minutes to fly through the defences; it was such a big place. It was a case of you were lucky or you were unlucky.' Jack recalls how he protected himself from the reality of losses. 'You kept your crew to yourself because if you started making mates with all the crews and then they went the next morning, you realised it more. Whereas you didn't notice it if you kept yourself to yourself. You didn't know them.'

John Chapman DFM, a Flight Engineer with No. 156 Squadron, who flew nine times to Berlin with the squadron during 1943, recalled at briefing the response from crews

to us. Many were the times you would know a crew or a particular person in another crew and he was there one day and the next day missing. In fact one or two were in the same billet as me and when they didn't come back one night, the next day their belongings were gone.' John Chapman's last operation with No. 156 Squadron took place in December 1943. He would not be in the same briefing as Dennis and Les on 1 January 1944 and wouldn't hear the 'Oh no, not again' on this occasion.

Dennis Mills

Dennis Mills was born in October 1923 in Newtown, Powys, Wales, where he lived out his youth prior to joining the Royal Air Force Volunteer Reserve. Dennis was destined to be an air gunner and trained in Defiants at No. 2 Air Gunnery School, prior to arrival at No. 156 Squadron early in 1943. With a Sergeant Ronald Stewart as his pilot, Dennis and his crew conducted their first operation on the night of 28 February 1943, attacking the U-boat facilities at Saint-Nazaire, one of 437 aircraft (5 losses) that caused substantial damage to the town and port. Over the next few months Dennis's logbook filled with brief details of his operations, as they flew as

"Jack Watson DFM recalled the first time he saw Berlin under attack, 'burning like mad, a huge red glow in the sky, and that was from fifty miles away.'"

when it became apparent that they were to go to Berlin again, 'A quite audible lull and then "Oh no, not again.' John Chapman, who flew on some of the same operations as Dennis Mills and Les Gill, recalled: 'We tended to be a family in our crew and thought it would never happen

part of Bomber Command's intensive spring, summer, and autumn campaigns of 1943. Included were attacks as part of the Battle of the Ruhr, a raid on Hamburg, long flights to Italian targets, and on the night of 17/18 August 1943 they took part in the famous raid against the German secret weapon establishment at Peenemünde. As autumn turned to winter, the crew edged past the thirty, then thirty-five, operations mark, and into November 1943 Dennis Mills became part of RAF Bomber Command's Battle of Berlin. On the nights of 18/19 November, 22/3 November and 23/4 November, Ronald Stewart piloted his crew to Germany's 'Big City'. Historians now view the middle of those three raids as the most effective against Berlin of the entire war. On the night of 16/17 December the crew found themselves, once more, attacking Berlin. Bomber Command lost twenty-five aircraft, mostly to German night fighters, on the raid (with a further twenty-nine Lancasters lost in either crashes or abandoned as crews met low cloud on their return to England). To date, Dennis Mills and his crew had managed to avoid any serious encounters with enemy aircraft. That would change on the night of 20/1 December 1943, during a raid to Mannheim.

DAVID MILLS

ROYAL AIR FORCE

PATH FINDER FORCE

Award of
Path Finder Force Badge

This is to certify that

1519562 FLIGHT SERGEANT MILLS, D.A.

who was reported missing on the 2nd day of

JANUARY 1944, is hereby

Permanently awarded the Path Finder Force Badge

Issued this 8th day of JANUARY in the year 1944. A.D.

Air Officer Commanding Path Finder Force.

Left: Dennis Mills's Path Finder Force Badge certificate.

Combat Report

No. 156 Squadron
Night 20/21 Dec 1943

Captain - F/L Stewart
Navigator - F/S Hudson
W/Operator - P/O Handley
F/Engineer - F/S Thorington
B/Aimer - F/L Fletcher
M/U/Gunner - F/S Mills
R/Gunner - F/L Horner

Target. Mannheim

Bomb Load

6x4 Flrs White.
1xFlr R/G. 1x T.I.M.
1xT.I.R L/B
1x4000 H.C 4x1000 C.f.
1xRed Spot Fire

Time Out 1714 hrs
Time In 2250 hrs

Landed. Bungay

On the night of Dec 20th 1943 a Lancaster III, A/C letter X of 156 Squadron,
captain F/L Stewart, was detailed as a Blind Marker Illuminator in an attack
on Mannheim.

Combat 1

On the homeward route at position 5018N. 0718E. at 2011 hrs, height 18000 ft,
heading 256M, our A/C was doing mild evasive action when the mid-upper gunner
sighted a Ju88 about 60° on starboard quarter at about 600 yds range. Mid-upper
gunner instructed pilot to corkscrew and the Ju88 was then sighted by rear gunner
about 10° on starboard quarter. The E/A opened fire at 300 yds range rendering our
rear turret U/S before rear gunner could reply. Rear gunner instructed captain to
turn to port and enemy A/C was lost to view. Pilot continued to corkscrew and
about 4 mins later the same E/A was sighted dead astern about 400 yds closing in
by the rear gunner who instructed the pilot to turn to port. E/A opened fire at
about 300 yds range, his fire passing underneath our starboard wing. The mid-
upper did not open fire as the E/A was invisible underneath.
        E/A closed in to 200 yds and disappeared below. Pilot then resumed
corkscrew action and 2 mins later the E/A was again sighted dead astern 30° down
at about 400 yds. Owing to corkscrew action the mid-upper was able to fire a short
burst but both guns jammed after 2 secs. No strikes were observed on the E/A. On
sighting the E/A on this attack the rear gunner instructed the pilot to turn to
port. The enemy's fire made a further hit on the rear turret and damaged the inner
engine nacelle and punctured the starboard tyre. E/A was then lost to view on the
starboard quarter.
        Corkscrew action was once more resumed and about 5 mins later the Ju88
was observed approx. the same position as in the previous attack. The rear gunner
instructed the pilot to turn to port. E/A closed in to 200 yds and opened fire,
his fire passing under the fuselage. E/A was then finally lost to view. E/A was
showing no lights, boozer was not fitter and fishpond was U/S. During the whole
of this action the W/operator was stationed in the astrodome but was unable to see
anything of combat.

Prevailing conditions. No flak or searchlights. 10/10ths cloud, tops 7,000 ft, no
moon. Starlit sky, visibility moderate. Scatter fires silhouetted us on the
port side.

Combat 2

On the homeward route at position 5022N. 0523E. 2043hrs, 16,000ft, heading 285M. the M/U/Gunner sighted an Me109 on S/B quarter 40° above at about 400 yds. Rear turret of our A/C had been put out of action by a previous encounter with a Ju88, and incendiary material was burning beneath the turret floor. Mid-upper gunner immediately instructed the pilot to corkscrew and then opened fire using sunscreen instead of sight, which was U/S, with 4 bursts of about 3 secs each. E/A closed in dead astern, and as the S/B wing of our A/C was down, the pilot made a slight turn to S/B then full turn to port. E/A then broke away to S/B.

About 30 secs later E/A came in on port quarter 30° above from 400 yds. M/U/Gunner opened fire again at 300 yds, the sight now being in order again. Strikes were observed on the enemy A/C. Our A/C continued to port turn, R/G observing E/A passing from port to S/B and seeing flashes coming from its engine as E/A disappeared.

E/A did not reappear and is claimed as damaged. During the whole of this combat the Me109 did not open fire. The W/Operator observed the combat from the astrodome.

Prevailing conditions. No flak or searchlights. Cloud 10/10ths, tops 7,000 ft, no moon, starlit sky, visibility moderate.

Rear Gunner. F/L Horner was trained at No. 9 A.G.S Llandwros and at No. 12 O.T.U Chipping Warden.
M/U/Gunner. F/S Mills was trained No.2 A.G.S Dalcross.

On 23/4 December and 29/30 December it was back to the 'Big City' once more for Dennis Mills. Then on New Year's Day Stewart's crew were yet again detailed to continue the unrelenting attack on Berlin. This would be their seventh trip to the German capital. It would also be their last.

Leslie Gill

On 16 May 1939 Leslie Gill received his Royal Air Force Boy Entrants Passing-Out Report. Out of the 159 fellow trainees in his entry, he was placed twenty-second, one of his instructors recording 'Has worked extremely well since transfer to this School. Very good practical worker. Has obtained very satisfactory results in all subjects.' The Flight Lieutenant Commanding 'C' Squadron, No. 3 Wing (Boys) No. 1 Electrical and Wireless School Cranwell, recorded that 'This Corporal Boy is keen and capable.'

At the outbreak of the war Leslie was with No. 207 Squadron, which was being used as a training unit, and in April 1940 the 'squadron' became part of No. 12 Operational Training Unit. In August 1941 Leslie joined No. 90 Squadron, and for the next few years he took up various operational and training duties.

Les remained with No. 90 Squadron until February 1942, followed by a spell at No. 1653 Conversion Unit, No. 1657 Conversion Unit, No. 199 Squadron, No. 27 OTU, No. 1656 Conversion Unit, No. 460 Squadron, and finally No. 156 Squadron.

By the end of 1943 Les had flown eight operations with No. 156 Squadron, three times to Frankfurt, once to Hanover, once to Leipzig, and three times to Berlin.

MICHAEL COLLINS

Left: Les Gill, married to Barbara in April 1941, with their son Michael, late 1942/3.

MICHAEL COLLINS

Les Gill, centre bottom, in what is considered to be a pre-war photograph.

Left: Bomb Doors Open. Les Gill, standing second from the left, with his crew at No. 460 Squadron, RAF Binbrook. Three other airmen in the picture would transfer with Les to No. 156 Squadron: Bill Robertson (centre), Bill Raper (far right), and Clarence Gynther (second from right). The crew was split up under tragic circumstances.

The pilot, Squadron Leader Carl Kelaher RAAF, on the left, and the air gunner Sergeant Arthur Rolfe, third from left, decided to fly with a new crew on a raid to Berlin on 3/4 September 1943.

They were shot down by a night fighter over Denmark with the loss of all on board. 'Jack' Chadwick-Bates, third from right, would remain with No. 460 Squadron as an air gunner but lose his life on the Nuremberg raid of 30/1 March 1944.

Combat Report

Night 8/9th October 1943
No. 156 Squadron
Lancaster III(Y)
A/C 'Y'/156
Bomb Load.
1 x 4000MC
6 x 1000MC
Target. Hannover

Crew:
Captain. F/S Royle
Navigator. F/S Gynther
W/Opr. F/S Gill
F/Engineer. F/O Raper
B/A. F/Gnr. F/O Robertson
M/U. Gnr. F/S Lumsden
Rear Gnr. F/S Murray

Time Out. 23.04hrs Time In. 03.38hrs Landed. Warboys

On the night of the 8/9th October 1943 Lancaster III(Y), A/C 'Y' of 156 Squadron, Captain F/S Royle, was detailed as a Supporter in the attack on Hannover.

On the way home at position 52.07N.08.02E., at 01.52hrs, height 24,000ft, an F.W.190 was identified and immediately reported, flying on reciprocal course, diving from S/B bow, (up 30degs), out of cloud. Range estimated at 300 yds.

The Lancaster was climbing at the time, but M/U. Gunner gave directions to dive to S/B. Captain complied, and the E/A opened fire in a one second burst, firing amber tracer from judged machine gun positions. This fire was inaccurate, and passed away on port side of our aircraft. E/A continued his dive, closing the range to 180 yds, and dived right over our aircraft, disappearing on the port quarter, down. It was not seen again.

Our aircraft's mid-upper turret had gone u/s during flight, and return fire could not therefore be made. E/A is confirmed by the T/Gnr. to have been a F.W.190, and note is made that its undercarriage was in a down position at the time of the attack

NORTH SEA

• Hamburg

Berlin

London

• Duisberg
• Cologne

Night raid on Berlin. No. 156 Squadron crews, eighteen in total, were tasked with acting as primary blind markers and blind markers on the night of 1/2 January 1944. Using their ground mapping 'H2S' radar equipment, they could 'see' through cloud and the darkness of the night and thereby assist with route marking to and from Berlin. Then, at the forefront of the attack itself, they could identify the target for subsequent markers and the Main Force bombers.

Squadron Leader Stewart, flying Lancaster MkIII JB703 GT-X, took off from RAF Warboys at 0033 hours.

Pilot:	Squadron Leader Ronald Stewart DFC
Navigator:	Flight Sergeant Raymond Hudson
Air Bomber:	Flight Sergeant Mervyn Fletcher DFC RAAF
Flight Engineer:	Flight Sergeant Frederick Thorington
Wireless Operator:	Pilot Officer Christopher Handley DFC
Mid-Upper Gunner:	Flight Sergeant Dennis Mills DFM
Rear Gunner:	Flight Lieutenant Cyril Horner DFC

Flying Officer Docherty, flying Lancaster MkIII JB476 GT-R, took off from RAF Warboys at 0038 hours.

Pilot:	Flying Officer Thomas Docherty
Navigator:	Pilot Officer Clarence Gynther RAAF
Air Bomber:	Flying Officer William Robertson RAAF
Flight Engineer:	Flying Officer William Raper RAAF
Wireless Operator:	Warrant Officer Leslie Gill
Mid-Upper Gunner:	Flight Sergeant William Lumsden DFM
Rear Gunner:	Flight Sergeant Jack Murray

At this stage of the war, RAF Bomber Command attacks were carefully planned, timed and coordinated assaults. Pathfinders, such as Ronald Stewart's and Thomas Docherty's crews, were allocated specific bombing and marking duties and the Main Force aircraft all had their allocated attack times. The aim was to focus the attacking force in time and space, and to overwhelm the defences and cause maximum destruction. The following narrative from the Bomber Command Night Raid Report No. 500 describes the detail of the operation.

Routemarking

On the outward route, primary blind markers and blind backers-up from 97 and 156 Squadrons were each to drop yellow TI* (LB) and 1 green steady flare at 52°50'N 08°50'E (16 miles S of Bremen): and primary blind markers, blind backers-up and special blind backers-up from 7, 83 and 405 Squadrons were to drop yellow TI (LB) at 52°37'N 12°20'E (18 miles NW of Brandenburg). On the way back primary blind markers and blind backers-up of 97 and 156 Squadrons were each to drop one green steady flare at

51°15'N, 12°37'E (11 miles SW of Leipzig); and primary blind markers, blind backers-up, and special blind backers-up of 7, 83 and 405 Squadrons were to drop one green steady flare at 50°30'N, 07°20'E (14 miles NW of Coblenz).

Method of Attack

Primary blind markers were to mark the aiming point with red TI dropping at the same time a bundle of release-point flares (red/green stars).

Blind backers-up, spread throughout the attack, were to keep the aiming point marked with greens and release-point flares; special blind backers-up were to do likewise with heavier salvoes. Visual backers-up were to aim greens at the estimated centre of all visible reds, early in the attack; later arrivals were to bomb on the centre of greens, adding 10 knots to the W/V set on bomb-sight. In either case they were to overshoot by 2 seconds. But if cloud rendered the TI invisible, they were to hold their greens, and bomb the release point flares on a heading of 171°Magnetic. Supporters were to bomb blindly if possible, otherwise release-point flares or the centre of reds. Main force aircraft were to aim at the centre of greens, or at release point flares on the heading prescribed for the backers-up.

Zero hour – 0300

Duration of attack: 0258 – 0312

Primary blind markers	22 Lancs at zero-2
Blind backers-up	12 Lancs at zero, zero+2, +4, +6(2), +7, +8(2), +9(2), +10 and +11
Special blind backers-up	5 Lancs at zero+1, +3, +5, +7 and +10
Visual backers-up	15 Lancs from zero to zero+11 (one per min. but 2 at zero, zero+1, and zero+6)
Supporters	33 Lancs at zero+2
Main Force	117 Lancs from zero to zero+4
	116 Lancs from zero+4 to zero+8
	115 Lancs from zero+8 to zero+12
	20 ABC aircraft throughout the attack
Marker Loads	
Primary blind markers	1x4 flares (R/G stars) + 4 red TI (2LB) + 2 yellow TI (LB)
Special blind backers-up	1x4 flares (R/G stars) + 4 green TI (2LB) + 2 yellow TI (LB)
Visual backers-up	6 green TI (3LB)

N.B. All primary blind markers and blind backers-up were to carry 2 green steady flares internally.

**Window was to be dropped at the rate of one bundle every minute to a point 40 miles from the target; 2 bundles every minute from that point to the target, and back; and one bundle every minute for the rest of the route home, until the supply was exhausted.

Diversions:

15 Mosquitoes were to carry out a feint attack on Hamburg, dropping red and green TI at zero – 26(6), -24(2), -23, -22, -21, -20, -19, -18, and -17. A direct run was to be made from 52°50'N, 08°50'E to Hamburg; during which Window was to be dropped at the rate of 3 bundles per minute.

Over the North Sea and the Dutch coast the bomber crews experienced broken cloud, three bombers fell to fighters, but once over the continent it rapidly developed into complete

initially carried out by the primary blind markers. (Returning No. 156 Squadron crews reported attacking between 0258 hours and 0314 hours.) But Bomber Command could

were lost to flak over the target, and there were 2 losses to fighters. On the return route a further 3 aircraft fell to fighters. One further aircraft was lost that night, believed not to be due to enemy action, reports coming in of a bomber exploding 50 miles east of Cromer, Norfolk. In return Bomber Command recorded 6 enemy aircraft believed destroyed. Analysis of the results of this specific raid was prevented owing to the cloud cover. For many of the crews that returned that night little did they realise that the following night they would once more be detailed to attack Berlin. 'Oh no. Not again!'

"Against the names of four crews in the No. 156 Squadron Operation Records Book was recorded 'This aircraft failed to return.'"

cloud cover, which continued until the target. Bomber Command estimated that nine aircraft were lost to ground fire en route to the target. Further aircraft fell to the German fighters, the spoof attack on Berlin having failed to draw the aerial defenders, Bomber Command recording a further eight losses on the approach to the target.

Crews attacking Berlin had to rely on the skymarking, with good marking

only record later that 13 of the detailed 29 backers-up reported an attack and only 7 of these released their flares, the supporters were late to the target, and the attack was scattered. The first crews to Berlin were confronted with accurate predicted flak, the cloud acting as a barrier to the searchlights. As the raid developed, German gunners sent up a barrage in the area around the release point flares. It was believed 2 aircraft

Against the names of four crews in the No. 156 Squadron Operation Records Book was recorded 'This aircraft failed to return.' There was a total loss of life, 28 airmen, including Dennis Mills and Les Gill.

Right: Dennis Mill's logbook. The person writing in the logbook has forgotten to realise the operation on which Dennis was lost took place in 1944.

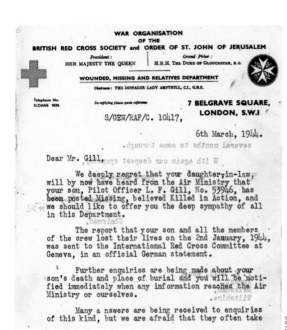

WAR ORGANISATION
OF THE
BRITISH RED CROSS SOCIETY and ORDER OF ST. JOHN OF JERUSALEM

President:
HER MAJESTY THE QUEEN

Grand Prior:
H.R.H. THE DUKE OF GLOUCESTER, K.G.

WOUNDED, MISSING AND RELATIVES DEPARTMENT

Chairman: THE DOWAGER LADY AMPTHILL, C.I., G.B.E.

Telephone No.
SLOANE 9696

In replying please quote reference

S/GEW/RAF/C. 10417,

7 BELGRAVE SQUARE,
LONDON, S.W.1

6th March, 1944.

Dear Mr. Gill,

We deeply regret that your daughter-in-law, will by now have heard from the Air Ministry that your son, Pilot Officer L. F. Gill, No. 53946, has been posted Missing, believed Killed in Action, and we should like to offer you the deep sympathy of all in this Department.

The report that your son and all the members of the crew lost their lives on the 2nd January, 1944, was sent to the International Red Cross Committee at Geneva, in an official German statement.

Further enquiries are being made about your son's death and place of burial and you will be notified immediately when any information reaches the Air Ministry or ourselves.

Many answers are being received to enquiries of this kind, but we are afraid that they often take

P.T.O.

MICHAEL COLLINS

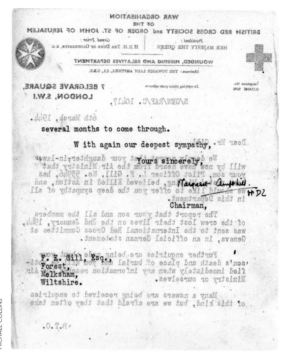

WAR ORGANISATION
OF THE
BRITISH RED CROSS SOCIETY and ORDER OF ST. JOHN OF JERUSALEM

7 BELGRAVE SQUARE,
LONDON, S.W.1

S/GEW/RAF/C. 10417,

6th March, 1944.

several months to come through.

With again our deepest sympathy,

Yours sincerely,

Margaret Ampthill
Chairman,

F. E. Gill Esq.,
"Forest",
Melksham,
Wiltshire.

P.T.O.

Left: 6 March 1944 letter from the War Organisation of the British Red Cross Society and Order of St John of Jerusalem to Les Gill's father.

Gerrard 9234

Casualty Branch,
77, Oxford Street,
London. W.1

P.412226/6/P.4.A.2.

16 February, 1944.

Sir,

I am commanded by the Air Council to inform you that they have with great regret to confirm the telegram in which you were notified that, in view of information now received from the International Red Cross Committee, your son, Flight Sergeant Dennis Arthur Mills, Royal Air Force, is believed to have lost his life as the result of the air operations on 2nd January, 1944.

The Committee's telegram, quoting official German information, states that your son and the six other occupants of the aircraft in which he was flying were killed on 2nd January. It contains no information regarding the place of their burial.

Although there is unhappily little reason to doubt the accuracy of this report, the casualty will be recorded as "missing believed killed" until confirmed by further evidence, or until, in the absence of such evidence, it becomes necessary, owing to lapse of time, to presume for official purposes that death has occurred. In the absence of confirmatory evidence death would not be presumed until at least six months from the date when your son was reported missing.

/The

C. Mills, Esq.,
"Rhoslyn",
Pool Road,
Newtown,
Montgomeryshire.

Left: 16 February 1944 letter from the Air Ministry Casualty Branch to Dennis Mills's parents.

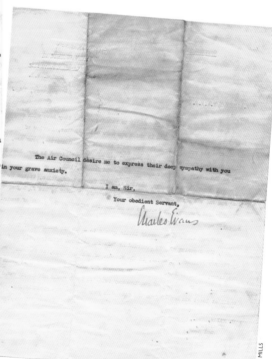

The Air Council desire me to express their deep sympathy with you in your grave anxiety.

I am, Sir,
Your obedient Servant,

Charles Evans

DAVID MILLS

Right: 19 January 1944 letter from Ronald Stewart's mother to Dennis Mills's father and transcript.

19th Jan 1944.

STN: GREENLOANING.
TEL: 202 BRACO.

FEDDAL,
BRACO,
PERTHSHIRE.

Dear Mr. Mills
Forgive me writing to you - but I wanted you to know how I share & sympathise in your anxiety about your son. Ronald my boy was in the plane too, so I know how you must have felt on receiving the Air Ministry telegram.
Ronald talked so much about the crew & I know what good friends they all were - that I got your address from the C.O. so that I could make contact & tell you how often I think of you & your family.
Any unofficial news I may receive I will most certainly send on to you - meantime we must go on hoping & praying that they have baled out somewhere & are safe.
Yours sincerely
Rita Falconar-Stewart

DAVID MILLS

19th Jan 1944

Dear Mr Mills
Forgive me writing to you but I wanted you to know how I share & sympathise in your anxiety about your son. Ronald my boy was in the plane too, so I know how you must have felt on receiving the Air Ministry telegram.
Ronald talked so much about the crew & I know what good friends they all were – that I got your address from the CO so that I could make contact & tell you how often I think of you & your family.
Any unofficial news I may receive I will most certainly send on to you – meantime we must go on hoping & praying that they have baled out somewhere & are safe.

Yours sincerely

Rita Falconar-Stewart

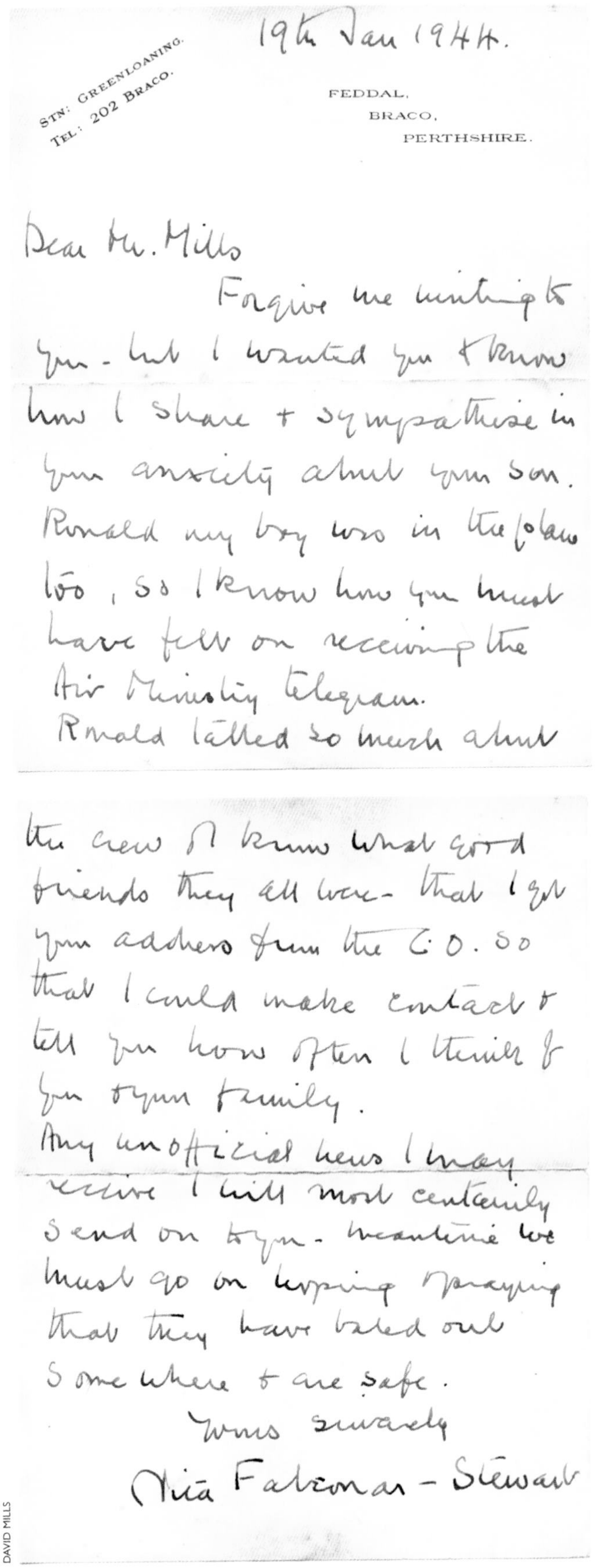

DENNIS ARTHUR MILLS DFM

Nationality: British
Rank: Flight Sergeant (Air Gnr)
Regiment/Service:
Royal Air Force
Unit: 156 Sqdn
Age: 20
Date of Death: 2 January 1944
Service No: 1509562
Grave/Memorial Reference:
7. J. 13.

LESLIE FRANK GILL

Nationality: British
Rank: Pilot Officer
(W.Op./Air Gnr)
Regiment/Service:
Royal Air Force
Unit: 156 Sqdn
Age: 23
Date of Death: 2 January 1944
Service No: 53946
Grave/Memorial Reference:
Coll. grave 5. L. 27-29.

For further details, see the Commonwealth War Graves Commission website: **www.cwgc.org**

Dennis Mills DFM

The recommendation for his Distinguished Flying Medal was made on 20 December 1943.

'**Flight Sergeant Mills has proved himself to be a very trustworthy and reliable Air Gunner throughout the 40 operational sorties he has undertaken against the enemy. His coolness when facing enemy opposition and his conduct as an operational gunner have always been of the highest order. Flight Sergeant Mills, by his outstanding devotion to duty, has made himself a very reliable member of an outstanding Pathfinder Force crew and is worthy of being strongly recommended for the award of the Distinguished Flying Medal.'**

Dennis's DFM was awarded with effect from 1 January 1944, the night he lost his life. ∎

Clockwise from left:
The original grave of 'F/Sjt' Dennis Mills DFM.

The grave of Les Gill at the Berlin 1939–45 War Cemetery.

Michael Collins at his father's grave in 2005.

A modern photograph of Dennis's grave at the Berlin 1939–45 War Cemetery.

With thanks to Dennis Mills's nephew David Mills, Les Gill's son Michael Collins, Len Traynor, John Chapman DFM, and Jack Watson DFM for their help with this chapter.

Thanks also to Robin Riley for his assistance. Robin runs the excellent www.156squadron.com website.

American Ace
over Normandy

Deemed essential to the success of the June 1944 Allied assault on the Normandy beaches and the subsequent break out into northern France and beyond was Allied air superiority over the battle area. In the run-up to the actual invasion, the Allied air forces were to keep up the attrition of the German Air Force both in the air and on the ground. Then, once the troops had landed, the air force was to provide a protective aerial umbrella. As part of the overall air plan Allied fighter pilots would seek out and destroy enemy aircraft in the sky and on their airfields prior to and after D-Day. One such fighter pilot who would distinguish himself in the Normandy air battle was Squadron Leader Henry 'Hank' Zary DFC.

AL BRANDON COLLECTION

By 1944 Hank Zary, an American citizen who had taken up the cause with the Royal Canadian Air Force, had already tangled with enemy fighters, while serving with No. 421 Squadron: on 10 July 1943 a Me109 damaged, similarly on 19 September 1943. On 8 May 1944 Hank would take the fight directly to the enemy, during an attack on Montdidier airfield.

PERSONAL COMBAT REPORT

DATE:	8th May 1944
SQUADRON:	421 Squadron
TYPE OF A/C:	Spitfire IX.B
TIME UP: DOWN:	0605-0815
TIME OF ATTACK:	Approx. 0730
PLACE OF ATTACK:	Montdidier
HEIGHT OF ENEMY:	On the ground on airdrome
OWN HEIGHT:	8,000 ft.
OUR CASUALTIES:	Nil
ENEMY CASUALTIES:	1 Ju.88 destroyed

Narrative: I circled airdrome at 8,000'; on the Montdidier a/d, five to seven enemy a/c observed dispersed in sandbagged bays on the south side of the a/d. The bays were sandbagged quite high on three sides. I dove out of the sun and opened fire on one of the e/a from about 800 yds. closing to 50 yds. Several long bursts were fired and strikes observed along port engine and wing and along fuselage up to the cockpit. Majority of strikes seen around center section of plane up front and port engine to the wing root. Large pieces were seen to fly off from frontal part of a/c. The e/a started smoking badly as I broke off the attack. Claim Ju.88 destroyed.
Saw F/O P.G. Johnson (421 Sqd.) destroy 1 Me.110. Me.110 crashed into field - small fire started and ammunition was exploding in enemy a/c.

Following the day of the Normandy assault itself, the Allies fought hard to extend the beachheads and provide space for 'Advanced Landing Grounds'; thus preventing long flights from English airfields. On 16 June 1944 the author of the No. 421 Squadron (RCAF) Operations Record Book wrote, 'The day for our own little invasion of the Continent has arrived. The Air Lift party took off at 14.15 hours in ten big Dakota transport aircraft and set down at B.2 at 15:20. The "Dak's" were escorted by Spits from our own Wing but it proved to be a very uneventful flight.' In fact, the pilots of the squadron (which formed part of 127 Wing) had been operating from B2 (the Advanced Landing Ground at Bazenville) in the days preceding the full movement of squadron personnel – a landing strip that had been cut from the French soil once the land had been overrun by the assaulting ground troops.

Over the next few days the squadron adjusted to the conditions. 'All roads are ankle deep in fine dust and every breath of wind blows clouds all over everyone and everything.' 'Don't know which is the worst, Jerry's bombs or our flak. At any rate it is very difficult to get sleeping

hours in.' Nevertheless No. 421 Squadron played its part in maintaining the air 'umbrella' over the Allied ground troops. On 28 June six of the squadron's Spitfires were sent to carry out a patrol of the front line. 'Huns were sighted.'

NATIONAL ARCHIVES OF CANADA PL 19872

Opposite page:
No. 421 Squadron, 1 June 1944, Hank Zary, fifth from right, top row.

Left: Ace fighter pilot Hank Zary.

PERSONAL COMBAT REPORT

DATE:	28th June, 1944
SQUADRON:	421
TYPE OF A/C:	Spit IX.B
TIME UP: DOWN:	1724-1824
TIME OF ATTACK:	1800
PLACE OF ATTACK:	Caen area
HEIGHT OF ENEMY:	7,000 ft.
OWN HEIGHT:	7,000 ft.
OUR CASUALTIES:	Nil
ENEMY CASUALTIES:	1 Me.109 Destroyed.

Narrative: I was flying Red 3 with 421 Squadron on a patrol. We were flying in a North Easterly direction towards Caen, when we spotted 14 plus Me.109's ahead of us flying in a South Westerly Direction. Two of the e/a were off to the right of us, the remainder to our left. I broke around to get behind the two e/a on our starboard which were flying line abreast. I got onto their tails at about 1,000 yds., range. I closed and opened fire at 600 yds., with one ring deflection, getting in about a 2 second burst. I closed to approximately 100 yds., and dead astern firing all the time. Strikes were observed on his tail and port wing. Black smoke poured from him and flashes - possibly further strikes could be seen through the smoke. Flames burst from his engine and he began to dive down well wreathed in flames. I then broke away to engage the second e/a but my number two was already making an attack on him. F/O Flood saw the combat and confirms that the e/a was diving down in flames. I claim 1 Me.109 destroyed.

Right: 13 August 1944, Supermarine Spitfire Mark IXs of No. 421 Squadron RCAF prepare to taxi out from their dispersals at B2/Bazenville, Normandy, for a routine dusk patrol.

IWM CL 782

Through July 1944 No. 421 Squadron continued in its struggle to protect the Allied ground forces from enemy aerial intervention, and to harass enemy transport, although poor weather hampered operations. On 23 July: 'The Wing was honoured by a visit from the Right Honourable Winston Churchill today and he gave a short speech during which he praised the work done by the Wing in particular and the RCAF in general.' On 25 July 1944 American bombers were due to carry out a massive bombardment of the German front line, at the western end of the battle front. To the east Allied fighters were protecting the flank of the bomber force. No. 421 Squadron's Operations Record Book recorded, '25.7.44: On the first armed recce of the day the squadron ran into 40+ Me 109's in the Rouen area.' The squadron pilots would claim 5 enemy aircraft destroyed, 1 probable and 3 damaged, but one of the squadron's pilots failed to return. Flying Officer George Cashion had lost his life.

PERSONAL COMBAT REPORT

DATE:	25th July 1944
SQUADRON:	421 Squadron
TYPE OF A/C:	Spit IX.B
TIME UP: DOWN:	1035-1144
TIME OF ATTACK:	1100
PLACE OF ATTACK:	Les Andelys area
HEIGHT OF ENEMY:	10-15,000 ft.
OWN HEIGHT:	10,000 ft.
OUR CASUALTIES:	1 Spit IX.B F/O G. Cashion (missing)
ENEMY CASUALTIES:	3 Me.109's Destroyed

Narrative: I was flying east leading 'B' Flight (Pink 5) in Les Andelys area at 10,000', when 40 plus Me.109's were sighed at 10-15,000 ft., on a reciprocal course. I broke to the right as e/a opened fire. After an orbit to starboard I followed two e/a who pulled up climbing-one of them turning to port and diving. I fired at the latter 2 second (m/g and cannon) saw strikes on starboard wing tip then e/a straightened out and dived gently. He then jettisoned his coupe-top and bailed out. The chute did not open. This e/a is claimed as destroyed.

I climbed to join Spits above. I saw Pink 3 (F/O Neil) fire at one Me.109 and saw strikes on fuselage and wing root. E/a then half rolled and went straight down glycol and black smoke streaming from him. Two Me.109's came down towards me, line astern, 50 deg. to starboard and I fired a 4 second burst (m/g and cannon) at second e/a. and saw a huge explosion in cockpit. E/a then disintegrated and fell straight down. This e/a is claimed as destroyed.

I climbed again to circling Spits above at 7-8,000 ft. Four e/a then came down flying in an easterly direction, apparently homeward bound. I fired at last e/a, who dived to the deck and I followed. I was out of ammo. But remained above and behind him reporting e/a's position and lack of ammo., to my Squadron leader. I then dived on the e/a anyhow. The e/a turned sharply to starboard to evade, apparently hit a tree - then stalled into the ground. Smoke from this burning e/a was confirmed by Pink (3) F/O. Neil, who replied to my request for confirmation.

This e/a is also claimed as destroyed. Cine gun used. Gyro sight fitted.

The Allied exploitation of their air superiority, executed by pilots such as Hank Zary, was certainly instrumental in the ultimate success of the Normandy invasion and break-out into France. For the advance to Germany there would be no let-up; the Allied air forces continuing to capitalise on their advantage. Following some leave in Canada in November, Hank Zary returned to the UK towards the end of the year, serving with No. 416 Squadron and then taking command of No. 403 Squadron. Into 1945 Hank would add to his tally of enemy aircraft taken out of the battle.

PERSONAL COMBAT REPORT

DATE:	21st April, 1945
SQUADRON:	403
TYPE OF A/C:	Spit XVI
TIME UP: DOWN:	1500-1650
TIME OF ATTACK:	1630
PLACE OF ATTACK:	Schnackenburg T.0800
HEIGHT OF ENEMY:	7,000 ft.
OWN HEIGHT:	3,000 ft.
OUR CASUALTIES:	Nil
ENEMY CASUALTIES:	1 Me.109 Destroyed.

Narrative: I was KAPOK leader of an Armed Recce in Parchim area, when returning, I sighted 2 Me.109's apparently attacking ground targets. They were climbing, when we gave chase. They climbed to about 7,000 ft. And I closed on the starboard aircraft telling F/O Leslie to take the port one. Closing to 600 yds., line astern, I opened fire with 4 second burst to 400 yds., strikes cutting a third of starboard wing and rudder off. Strikes were also observed on the cockpit and the aircraft crashed out of control. F/O A.A. Roy confirms this report. Gyro sight and cine camera used.

I claim one Me.109 destroyed.

PERSONAL COMBAT REPORT

DATE:	April 25th, 1945
SQUADRON:	403
TYPE OF A/C:	Spitfire XVI
TIME UP: DOWN:	1545-1729
TIME OF ATTACK:	1630-1640
PLACE OF ATTACK:	Hagenow A/D & Schwerin A/D
HEIGHT OF ENEMY:	On Ground
OWN HEIGHT:	8000' - 0'
OUR CASUALTIES:	Nil
ENEMY CASUALTIES:	1 Me.262 Damaged -
	1 Ju.88 Damaged on Ground

Narrative: I was leading a section of four Kapok White a/c - climbed to 9000 ft. West of Hegnow A/D then dove down out of sun across A/D and giving a 7-8 second burst on Me.262 seeing it covered in strikes but no flames appeared. Climbed away and then led my section down onto Schwerin A/D together with F/L Foster leading other section of 4 a/c. I then climbed east of A/D to 8-9000 ft. Dove again across northern part of field and firing rest of cannon at Ju.88 - ran out of cannon and used machine gun seeing few strikes on wing and fuselage. Gyro sight fitted and Cine-gun used.

I claim 1 Me.262 and 1 Ju.88 as damaged.

Hank Zary ended the war as an 'Ace', and a true hero of the air war in Europe. Tragically his life would be cut short by pleurisy, and he died on 11 February 1946, at the age of 27.

Hank Zary's Distinguished Flying Cross: 'This officer is a most distinguished fighter whose keenness to engage the enemy has always been apparent. In July 1944, he took part in an engagement against a superior force of enemy fighters, three of which he shot down. This officer has completed a large number of sorties and has destroyed six enemy aircraft.' ∎

Most Excellent Performance

On the night of 29/30 August 1944 RAF Bomber Command despatched two large forces to attack the distant targets of Stettin (402 Lancasters and 1 Mosquito) and Königsberg (189 Lancasters). The raids caused severe damage and loss of life on the ground, but the bomber force paid a price: 23 Lancasters lost on the Stettin raid and 15 Lancasters lost on the Königsberg operation. Many of the airmen in these aircraft lost their lives, but in a No. 460 Squadron Lancaster the extraordinary determination of the pilot ensured his crew would survive.

Of the twenty-four No. 460 Squadron Lancasters that flew on the raid of 29/30 August 1944, two failed to return to RAF Binbrook. Flying Officer K. Humphries RAAF survived the loss of his aircraft, which came down in the Baltic Sea, along with three other members of his crew. The three other airmen in Humphries's Lancaster lost their lives. In the other No. 460 Squadron Lancaster that failed to return that night Flying Officer Peter Aldred's 'most excellent performance' ensured the survival of his entire crew.

REPORT ON LOSS OF AIRCRAFT ON OPERATIONS

AIRCRAFT   Lancaster III, No. PB379 'E2' of 460 Squadron
DATE OF LOSS   29/30 August 1944
TARGET   Stettin
CAUSE OF LOSS   The aircraft was hit by flak when outbound, and by falling bombs over the target, resulting in fairly severe damage. Both incidents were contributory to fuel shortage.
POSITION OF LOSS   Aircraft landed at Kalmar, in Sweden.
SPECIAL EQUIPMENT CARRIED   H2S, Fishpond, A.G.L.T.
INFORMATION FROM   F/Sgt. McNab D. navigator
Sgt. Whaling R. Wireless Operator
Sgt. Troth P.L. Flight Engineer
F/Sgt. Allcot R.J. Air Bomber
F/O Rice D.A. Mid Upper Gunner
F/Sgt. Jackson A.J.R. Rear Gunner

All on 8th operation

The W/Op., F/Eng, A/B and M/U/G were interrogated together, the Nav. and R/G were interviewed separately on two different occasions.

REMAINDER OF CREW   Pilot and Captain F/O Aldred P.M.N. on 9th operation. In hospital in Sweden.

ROUTE: Binbrook - 5530N 0500E - 5650N 0314E - 5626N 1235E - 5518N 1445E - 5340N 1508E - TARGET - 5320N 1420E - 5330N 1400E - 5430N 1400E - 5615N 1250E - 5620N 0800E - 5520N 0500E .

Narrative: The Lancaster took off from Binbrook about 2130 hours with a load consisting of a 4,000lb H.C. bomb and incendiaries to attack Stettin. Flak was encountered on the west coast of Jutland and half way across Denmark. On the latter occasion a bump was felt as if the bomb-bay had been hit, and although no damage was apparent immediately, it was appreciated afterwards that No. 2 port fuel tank was hit so that the contents drained. It seems probable that the H2S scanner was affected, certainly the Navigator was unable to use it subsequently. The A.G.L.T. fitting outside the Rear Turret was also holed.

Just before the east coast of Jutland was reached 460/E2 was engaged in combat by an enemy fighter. The enemy fighter, which came in from the port quarter up, is believed not to have fired. The Lancaster was corkscrewing at the time, and the Mid Upper Gunner, who saw the fighter, fired a series of bursts. The Rear Gunner was observing an AGL(T) contact on the beam. This contact, later seen to be a Lancaster, gave no Type Z response, presumably because it was at too great an angle off astern.

On approaching Bornholm the Navigator found that they were some 2 minutes ahead of E.T.A., so the Pilot decreased the speed slightly to get into phase. Flak was encountered over Bornholm and again on approaching the north German coast (flakships). The aircraft was now at about 18,000ft. and reached the coast on time. The run in to Stettin began, and after a while instructions from the Master Bomber were picked up to bomb at 12 to 13,000 feet instead of at the briefed height of 16 to

Left: Flight Lieutenant P.N. Aldred.

18,000 ft., so that the Pilot began to lose height. The night was dark, the moon having gone down; there was about 6/10ths cloud (scattered stratus) above the aircraft.

The Air Bomber could see fires burning in Stettin but was unable to pick out the exact aiming-point, so he told the Pilot to orbit to port, and to make another run. The second run was successful, in spite of being coned by searchlights and of considerable predicted heavy flak, bombs being released from 12,500 ft. at 0209 hrs. The Lancaster continued flying straight and level for the photographic run and the order to close bomb-doors was given, when the aircraft was hit by falling bombs. The Rear Gunner had noticed three Lancasters flying overhead at perhaps 16 to 18,000 feet and saw a 4,000lb. bomb, dropped by one of them, fall past. 460/E2 was caught by the edge of a scatter of falling incendiaries.

The aircraft was hit by about 12 4-lb incendiaries none of which ignited. One was found inside the fuselage, about half of another was lying in the Wireless Operator's compartment. A third came through the windscreen, hit the Pilot's right hand which was crushed and almost severed, damaged the control column, smashed the

THE ALDRED FAMILY

Above: The crew of No. 460 Squadron's PB379 in Sweden, minus their skipper, Peter Aldred (who was in a Swedish hospital). From left to right: Bob Jackson, Don McNab, Sandy (Rodney) Allcott, Dave Rice, Mike Whalan, and Johnny Troth. On their return to the UK the crew were able to report on the bravery of their skipper.

flap-lever right off, at the same time applying full flap, and came to rest in the Air Bomber's compartment. No. 1 starboard tank was holed by another which fell right through it, while a fifth lodged in the wing by the same tank, and a sixth remained stuck in the wing near the starboard aileron controls. It is also believed that a further bomb jammed in the hinge of the starboard flap. A seventh bomb hit and severed the ammunition and hydraulic lines to the rear turret, near the door. The turret happened to be pointing round on the beam, when the hydraulics went dead. An eighth bomb was found subsequently, lying near the rest bed. In the cockpit, the P.4 compass had been smashed, probably by the third of the bombs listed above, and the D.R. compass was also unserviceable.

The Pilot lost consciousness momentarily and the aircraft slideslipped down to port to about 9,000 ft., but the Pilot, helped by the Flight engineer, managed to regain control and the aircraft came out to the south of the target-area. The Pilot warned the crew to put on their 'chutes. The bombing course was maintained to get clear of the target, and the aircraft then turned north, more heavy flak being encountered, and it is believed that splinters struck the aft part of the fuselage. The engines had not been damaged in any of these incidents and the aircraft was making about 100 m.p.h. at 2650 revs. And +5boost with full flap on.

The Pilot was severely shocked and bleeding badly - his right hand being largely crushed to pulp. The Air Bomber rendered first aid, applying a tourniquet which was released at 20-minute intervals, and administering morphia. The Pilot was also wrapped in blankets and given all the available hot tea from the thermos flasks. In spite of his pain, he insisted that he could fly the aircraft back to Woodbridge, encouraging the rest of the crew for the remainder of the sortie and glossing over his own injury.

A fuel check showed that No.2 port tank and No.1 starboard tank were both empty, but the Flight Engineer was uncertain if all the gauges were registering correctly. No.3 port tank had been hit by flak splinters. The Pilot's R/T had become u/s, the H2S was also dead. In view of the fuel shortage it was now decided to make for Sweden, and course was set for Bornholm. The incendiary containers and one gun from the rear turret were jettisoned. The engines began to heat up because of the flaps being jammed fully on, but it was possible to maintain height at between 9 and 10000ft. and there was no further trouble.

Eventually Sweden was reached north of Bornholm and the aircraft headed up the east coast towards the lights of a town. The aircraft then circled over the coast of Oland at 9 to 10000ft. keeping the lights in view until dawn was approaching. The Navigator's maps were torn up and thrown out over the Baltic; a message was sent on the international frequency asking for permission to land, for landing instructions and for an ambulance and medical attention to be made available. No reply was picked up, but the message was evidently received as an ambulance was waiting when the aircraft landed. The Pilot was by now in a very bad way but insisted that he could land the aircraft.

Broken cloud was forming, and began to move inland. Sufficient fuel remained for only about 20 minutes flying, so the Pilot lost height to about 2000 feet and watched for the most suitable looking field intending to do a crash-landing. The field he chose turned out to be Kalmar aerodrome, so he made a wide circuit and came in to make a perfectly good wheels landing. The crew had taken up crash position except for the Air Bomber and Flight Engineer who stayed with the Pilot.

Later, the Engineer was allowed to return to the aircraft to patch up the holes in the wings sufficiently to prevent any further damage. He found that the flap controls had been so damaged by the falling incendiary that it would have been quite impossible to get the flaps up while the aircraft was airborne.

THE ALDRED FAMILY

Interrogator's comment
Attention is drawn to the Pilot's most excellent performance in bringing his aircraft safely to land in neutral territory, in spite of the severe injury he had sustained and of the considerable damage to his aircraft.

27 December 1944.

Note: The 'K' report refers to 'A.G.L.T.' and 'AGL(T). This stands for the Automatic Gun-Laying Turret, radar aimed to assist firing in total darkness. Codenamed 'Village Inn'. ∎

Extraordinary Fortune

You have managed to lift your explosive-laden bomber from the runway, survived the long flight over the cold and churning North Sea. Managed to dodge the enemy's fighters, and the flak guns seeking to blow you into oblivion over a target. You may just have managed to avoid a collision with other bombers as they funnelled into a target, or seen 'friendly' bombs fall within inches of your aircraft; indeed some may have actually hit and torn pieces from your bomber. For the return flight your aircraft may be damaged; indeed members of the crew may be injured, some fatally. The icy North Sea is once more beneath and you pray you do not have to ditch. You cross the English coast. But the danger is far from over. Your base, and the surrounding area, may be shrouded in thick fog. Fuel may be running low. You simply have to get the aircraft down, somewhere.

On the night of 21/2 December 1944, after a long ten-hour flight to attack Politz, near Stettin, RAF Bomber Command No. 9 Squadron Lancaster pilot Flying Officer 'Curly' Read found his home station of RAF Bardney, Lincolnshire, covered by thick fog. Time was running out. In the rear turret sat Sergeant Jack Linaker.

Although Jack Linaker had initially been called up to the Royal Artillery, he had stayed working within the steel industry, a reserved occupation. But Jack already held an ambition to fly.

When I was living in Northampton I used to bike to Sywell aerodrome, where I saw Amy Johnson and Alan Cobham's circus. I always wanted to fly. They had an instructor there by the name of Rose and he used to turn this aircraft inside out. Two things I wanted to do, I wanted to fly and I wanted to be a champion cyclist.

While working at the furnaces in Kettering, Northamptonshire, Jack volunteered for the air force and was put down for flight engineer training. He still had to overcome the problem of being in a reserved occupation. 'I contacted RAF Reading and told them they would have to call me up as I was going to refuse to work and would be put in gaol. Within a fortnight I was called up and sent down to Wales to do my initial training.'

To begin with Jack was attached to the RAF regiment until air crew came up. Then in 1942, 'All of a sudden they were looking for volunteers to be air gunners. I had already passed for aircrew so was put forward and went to London. I went before the board and told them I had already passed for flight engineer. They told me I was in.'

Crewing Up

Following his initial training Jack was sent to the air gunners' school, at Andreas, Isle of Man, and from there to No. 29 Operational Training Unit, at RAF Brunting-thorpe, to crew up.

We all gathered in a room. The first chap I met was 'Bunny' Rothwell. He came to me and said, 'here I've got a pilot and he wants a crew and he wants the most pissy-arsed crew he can get'. He knew I liked a drink. He said he wanted to be the mid-upper gunner and I said I'd be

JACK LINAKER

Jack Linaker, on the left. By the time the war came Jack Linaker already had numerous cycling trophies and medals to his name, having raced all over Britain.

happy to be the rear gunner. That's how I got crewed up with our pilot 'Curly' Read. Soon as we got crewed up, the first word was 'to the pub tonight'. We went and had a few pints. When we were in the crew together there was no 'yes sir, no sir, three bags full'. We knew that the pilot was the boss, he was the bus driver, he gave the orders, except if the aircraft was attacked the air gunner was the bloke telling them what to do.

The crew gelled at RAF Bruntingthorpe, and then went on to a Heavy Conversion Unit at RAF Winthorpe, picking up a flight engineer and developing their teamwork on a

Winthorpe and whether they got out or not I don't know.'

Following a spell at No. 5 Lancaster Finishing School at RAF Syerston, Jack and his crew were posted to No. 9 Squadron at RAF Bardney, Lincolnshire, in September 1944. The squadron had a reputation for carrying out special operations requiring very accurate bomb aiming, and Jack put their posting down to the achievements of his bomb aimer in training.

We arrived at Bardney and the place was almost deserted. Somebody found us a billet and we went to the Sergeants' Mess, wanting to know where everybody was, 'Shhh, top

Right: Lymne 1942. Jack Linaker with the RAF regiment, the camp adjutant's runner, at the back third from the right.

JACK LINAKER

four-engine bomber flying Stirlings, or, as Jack puts it, 'the abortion of the air force'. During his time at Bruntingthorpe and Winthorpe Jack witnessed two incidents in which the perils of training became clear. 'At OTU this chap came in and he hadn't got his wheels down. I've never seen anybody get out of the aircraft so quick – it all went up in flames. I saw one crash at

secret, they're in Russia.' They had gone to bomb the battleship Tirpitz. In the evening we went straight down to the pub, the Jolly Sailor, and everybody in the village knew where they were. On returning from Russia the crews bought back vodka in condoms, and lots of Russian money. One airman picked up a 'bit of stuff' in Nottingham one night and paid her in Russian money!

Operations

On 5 October 1944 the crew prepared to make their first flight over Germany, part of a 227 Lancaster and 1 Mosquito force sent to Wilhelmshaven.

It was a daylight raid and we had fighter escort. We were going in to bomb and we had the target all lined up. The flak was coming up but no German fighters. The mid-upper gunner could see everything and suddenly he said, 'Oh my God, we've been hit.' A Lanc had flown over and dropped a J-type cluster on the starboard outer engine, and a fire started. The Flight Engineer managed to put

back, me and Bunny, we got alongside of Vic Willis and said, 'Listen, if you can't press that tit first time, we'll come and press it for you. No going round twice.'

It was not until the night of 22/3 November that Jack next flew on operations.

We went to Trondheim Fjord, after the U-boat pens. We got there all right and they started throwing the flak up, no night fighters. The wireless operator, Mac, said 'stand-by'. We flew around the outside of the flak. Then 'standby' and then again 'standby' and again 'standby', then all of

Left: Jack's logbook entries for the raids of 5 October 1944 and 6/7 october 1944.

the fire out and feathered the engine, so we went straight in and dropped the bombs. The mid-upper said there were bits flying off the aircraft. All I could see was the sea and I said. 'For Christ's sake don't ditch, we'll bale out over land.' We got the aircraft back, we were the last one, we had a Lockheed Lightning escort us back to Bardney. When we got there we had to make a flapless landing and we were all in crash positions, and as we landed the ambulance came up the runway. We all walked out the aircraft, with thumbs up, nobody hurt.

On the night of 6/7 October the crew were detailed to attack Bremen, part of a 246 Lancaster and 7 Mosquito force.

When we got to Bremen, I can always remember, flares went down, then the rest of it [markers]. I'm not kidding, and don't know whether I should say it or not, but it was the most beautiful sight I'd seen, the colours. I never thought about the fact that down there people were being killed. The next thing, we were going in to bomb, and Vic Willis, the bomb aimer, was on the intercom, 'left, left, steady, right, right, steady, steady, go round again'. We'd missed the target. We went around again and this time dropped the bombs. When we were

a sudden he said 'Oh Jesus, I've read the flimsy wrong, it's "abandon the raid".' Now we hadn't got enough petrol to get back to Bardney, so we landed at Wick, Scotland. We went down the town and it was 'dry'. You had to buy a meal to get a drink!

On the night of 17/18 December Curly Read's crew were part of a 280 Lancaster and 8 Mosquito force sent to Munich. Four Lancasters were lost on the raid.

Before we got there a Mossie [Mosquito] was following us and I said to Curly Read, 'If he don't clear off I am going to open up on him.' You never knew, the Germans could put up our aircraft. Anyhow I gave him a few more seconds and then he buggered off. We got to Munich and I saw aircraft going down. It was a nine-hour flight to Munich and back and as rear gunner I was supposed to rotate my turret, searching, all the time.

Crash

Following an uneventful raid to Gdynia on the night of 18/19 December, a 9 hour 50 minute flight, the next time the crew were detailed for operations was on 21 December 1944, to attack the synthetic oil refinery at Pölitz, close to Stettin.

CHAPTER FOURTEEN

Right: Jack Linaker's logbook recording the fateful night of 21/2 December 1944.

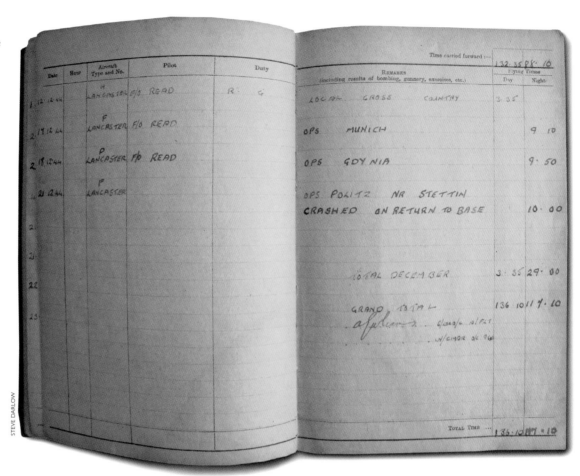

STEVE DARLOW

The air gunners had their own briefing and then you would go into the main briefing. We knew the target when we got there. Bazin was the Wing Commander. 'Gentlemen, tonight you'll be going to Stettin. It's a very important target, it's the oil refineries.'

Everytime we went on an op we would stand outside the aircraft, have a cigarette and I would get the third light. We would always say we were going to get the chop that night, but this was the only occasion when we didn't say it. We took off normally and everything was OK until we came across the flak. The bomb aimer said he'd hit the target and on the way back everything was more or less all right, until we reached England. The next thing we hear is that the drome, Bardney, was fog bound and we would have to go and land at a FIDO [Fog Investigation and Dispersal Operation] airfield — Coningsby. The flight engineer said, and I don't know why, that we hadn't got enough petrol to get to Coningsby. I often wonder why he said that, because as the crow flies Bardney to Coningsby is not far. Curly Read called the

control tower and asked if it was possible to make a landing at Bardney, and could they throw up Verey lights. We went round and came in pretty low but overshot. So we started to go round again and the next thing 'BANG'. Someone later said that we had hit a tree. I was in the rear turret, which broke off, and it went round and round and round. I'd got the back doors open ready for when we landed, and I fell out right into a potato field. I had no boots, I was covered in mud, and I walked towards where I thought the aircraft was, about 200 yards. I came across Bunny Rothwell and asked if he was all right. He replied 'Yeh.' Then I saw the bomb aimer Vic Willis stagger out of the wreckage, and he just fell straight down. How he managed to stagger out I don't know.

The crew of No. 9 Squadron Lancaster I PD213 WS-F

Pilot:	Flying Officer J. A. Read
Flight Engineer:	Sergeant E. A. White
Navigator:	Sergeant N. F. J. Featherstone

Bomb Aimer:	Flight Sergeant V. S. Willis
Wireless Operator:	Flight Sergeant D. McArdle
Mid-Upper Gunner:	Sergeant H. B. Rothwell
Rear Gunner:	Sergeant W. J. W. Linaker

When Jack got closer, it was clear that Vic Willis was dead, owing to the injuries to the back of his head. Jack pulled a parachute and covered his crewmate. Along with Bunny Rothwell, they scoured the wreckage looking for their other crewmates.

We then saw the navigator, who was also injured but not in a life-threatening way, and the wireless operator, who had cuts to the face. Then I came across our flight engineer, who was just lying down, dead.

But where was Curly Read, the pilot. He was nowhere to be seen, certainly not in the immediate vicinity of the aircraft. Eventually he was found, about 300 yards from the wreckage.

He had gone straight through the canopy and was still strapped in to his seat, quite a distance from the aircraft. He was unconscious having suffered a fractured skull, but he was alive. An ambulance came but got bogged down, so when another one arrived, and stayed on the road, Bunny and I helped get the others in.

On the way back to the airfield, Jack asked if he could be taken to the Officers' Mess, prior to sick bay, as he was desperate for a cup of tea. 'We walked in and the WAAF nearly fainted when she saw the state of us.' Jack was cleaned up in the station sick bay prior to a transfer to Sleaford for further medical examinations. Apart from having to deal with some burns and considerable bruising, Jack could consider himself extremely fortunate to have survived. He returned to the squadron on Christmas Day and was sent on survivor's leave.

After two weeks Jack returned to No. 9 Squadron, along with Bunny Rothwell, both prepared to act as 'spare bods'. Jack was fortunate to be teamed up with an experienced pilot, Ray Harris, whose previous gunner had been injured. Jack would see out the war in the rear of an aircraft piloted by a man for whom he had high respect, and who had already completed one tour, having begun piloting Lancasters at the age of 19. On their first operation

the call came that the raid was to be abandoned and they had to return to the UK with their 12,000lb 'Tallboy' bomb – they were valuable items and not to be ditched. As a precaution, Ray Harris took his crew to Woodbridge. 'It was a crash drome and we decided to land there because of our weight.' After a successful landing the crew found themselves being briefed by an American major.

He said, 'You mean to say you went all the way to Germany and came back with one bloody bomb and you never dropped it.'

'Yes.'

'Bloody Hell! With one bomb and you came all the way back?'

'Yes.'

'Right. You in that jeep, you in that jeep, we're going to see this.'

We went to where our kite was; they were just opening up the bomb bay. The American major looked up.

'Jesus Christ Almighty. You mean to say you sit on that much dynamite!'

The remainder of Jack's operational life passed relatively uneventfully, his last operation being to Heligoland on 19 April 1945. At the end of the war in Europe, Jack certainly did not shy away from the chance to celebrate. 'On VE Day we went to Nottingham; wine, women and song.'

We decided to put the Officers' Mess and Sergeants' Mess money together and invite the people of Bardney village to celebrate. Everything was free. Everyone was half-cut. There were blown-up condoms floating round like balloons. I tried to post a hurricane light home to my mother. The next thing I woke up and I was never again in such a state in my whole life as I was then. ∎

BRIAN MOSSEMENEAR

Left: The memorial at Bardney with the inscription, 'IX Squadron R.A.F. In memory of all ranks killed or missing 1939 – 1945'

On Christmas Day 1944 the American Eighth Air Force sent hundreds of heavy bombers to attack numerous communication centres and rail bridges, through which German supplies and reinforcements were passing to a growing 'bulge' in the mountainous Ardennes region of Belgium. Accompanying the bomber airmen were hundreds of their 'little friends', including pilots of the crack 56th Fighter Group.

Thunderbolt Fury

Right: Memorial at Boxted airfield, near Colchester, Essex, home of the 56th Fighter Group from April 1944.

STEVE DARLOW

It had been just over a week since the German land offensive was launched underneath the protective canopy of the poor weather conditions, and persistent fog, which had neutralised Allied air superiority. But on Christmas Eve, with the German advance faltering at the Meuse River, with their ammunition in short supply, and with fuel supplies drying up, it seemed as if the 'Battle of the Bulge' was turning in the Allies' favour. The weather had improved, and Allied airmen were now playing their part in supporting their colleagues on the ground. The heavy bombers were sent out to blast the supply routes to the battle area and the fighter pilots were tasked with protecting the armadas of B-17 Flying Fortresses and B-24 Liberators. One group of 'little friends' belonged to the 56th Fighter Group, and that day they would be in the midst of aerial combat. At the conclusion of the mission six of them would lay claim to the destruction of eight enemy aircraft.

By December 1944, the 56th Fighter Group, flying P-47 Thunderbolts, had already established a reputation as a fierce aerial combat unit. On 23 December 1944 the unit's pilots had claimed an extraordinary 32 enemy aircraft destroyed, which took it past the figure of 800 enemy aircraft eliminated in air combat and strafing attacks, the first American fighter group to do so. Two days later, more Messerschmitt 109s and Focke-Wulf 190s would fall to the guns of six of the 56th's pilots.

On the morning of 25 December, the 56th Fighter Group despatched 50 P-47s, taking off at 0925 hours, then heading east. The Group's Mission Summary Report for 25 December recorded an estimated 50–60 single-engine enemy aircraft seen 'in Bonn Koblenz area 1130 25/33,000 ft. They were evidently headed for the Bombers. Group forced them to drop belly tanks in ensuing combat. Some split and ran out; main body stuck together and hit the deck.'

56TH FIGHTER GROUP CLAIMS - 25 DECEMBER 1944

1 FW190	destroyed,	Lt. W.D. Clark,	61st Sq.
1 ME109	destroyed,	Capt Jackson,	62nd Sq.
2 ME109s	destroyed,	Lt Daley,	62nd Sq.
2 ME109s	destroyed,	F.O Sharbo,	62nd Sq.
1 ME109	destroyed,	Lt, Batson,	63rd Sq.
1 ME109	destroyed,	Capt. Hart,	63rd Sq.

CALLSIGNS

61st Fighter Squadron	Whippet (A Group),	Household (B Group)
62nd Fighter Squadron	Platform (A Group),	Icejug (B Group)
63rd Fighter Squadron	Daily (A Group),	Yorker (B Group)

HEADQUARTERS SIXTY FIRST FIGHTER SQUADRON

AAF Station F-150, APO 558
U.S. Army
Encounter Report 8 A.F. FO # 1451-A
1st Lt. William D. Clark, Jr.   Whippet Blue 3

a. Combat (air)
b. 25 December 1944
c. 61st Fighter Squadron, 56th Fighter Group
d. 1130 hours
e. Cologne
f. CAVU
g. FW-190
h. FW-190 destroyed (air)

i. I was flying Whippet Blue 3 when the squadron leader and my flight leader had trouble so I was ordered to take over the squadron. I led us over Cologne and circled once at 35,000 ft. Trying to give top cover for some 62nd ships below. I saw several aircraft split 's' for the deck about this time and on looking further saw 5 or 6 FW-190's below in a rough Lufberry with P-47's. As 3 190's were getting in position to bounce the yellow-tailed 47's I decided to enter the fight. As I rolled over to go down, one of the 190's split 's'd for the deck but apparently the other two did not see me. I made a pass on a 190 and when I opened up he lit up like a Christmas tree. Then I fired again and saw a burst of flame. I figured he was through so I quit firing and climbed back to altitude with my wingman, Lt. Hines. I believe the pilot was killed as I saw no chute. I claim one FW-190 destroyed.

j. 452 rds .50 cal API.

Above:
William D. Clark, Jr.

William D. Clark, Jr.,

William D. Clark, Jr.,
1st Lt., Air Corps.

Supporting Statement: I was flying Lt. Clarks' wing in the engagement on 25 Dec 1944. We were giving top cover to some 62nd ships below us. When 3 FW-190's were getting into position to make a pass on the P-47's, Lt. Clark dove into the fight; I followed at about a 500 yard distance. The FW started a slight turn to the right and I saw strikes completely covering it - then a burst of flame. When I passed the FW it was burning and his prop was windmilling. The pilot did not try to bail out; he was undoubtedly killed. We then climbed back to 34,000, our altitude. I confirm one FW-190 destroyed by Lt. W.D. Clark.

Luther P Hines, Jr.,

Luther P Hines, Jr.,
1st Lt., Air Corps.

Right:
William C. Daley.

HEADQUARTERS SIXTY SECOND FIGHTER SQUADRON

AAF Station F-150, APO 558
U.S. Army
Personal Combat Report
VIII Air Force F.O. No. 1451-A

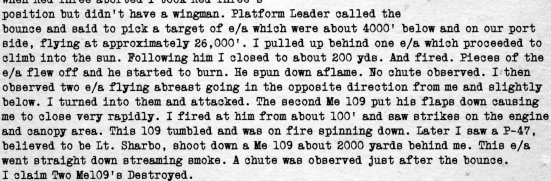

a. Combat (air)
b. 25 December 1944
c. 62nd Fighter Squadron
d. Approx. 1130 hours
e. Vicinity Bonn/Koblenz Area
f. Contrails persistent at 26/27,000'.
   Slight ground haze.
g. Me 109's
h. Two Me 109's claimed Destroyed.

i. I was flying Platform Red Four position. When Red Three aborted I took Red Three's position but didn't have a wingman. Platform Leader called the bounce and said to pick a target of e/a which were about 4000' below and on our port side, flying at approximately 26,000'. I pulled up behind one e/a which proceeded to climb into the sun. Following him I closed to about 200 yds. And fired. Pieces of the e/a flew off and he started to burn. He spun down aflame. No chute observed. I then observed two e/a flying abreast going in the opposite direction from me and slightly below. I turned into them and attacked. The second Me 109 put his flaps down causing me to close very rapidly. I fired at him from about 100' and saw strikes on the engine and canopy area. This 109 tumbled and was on fire spinning down. Later I saw a P-47, believed to be Lt. Sharbo, shoot down a Me 109 about 2000 yards behind me. This e/a went straight down streaming smoke. A chute was observed just after the bounce. I claim Two Me109's Destroyed.

William C. Daley

William C. Daley, 0430790. 1st Lt., Air Corps

Armament Report
Lt. William C. Daley   44-19792   768 rounds API

'. . . we were in a dog-fight over Cologne. My leader and I dove toward the Northeast section of the town and saw a yellow tail P-47 shoot down an Me109. The 109 was climbing at a steep angle into the sun and exploded as he was being shot at . . .'

Arthur J. Martin, Jr.
Arthur J. Martin, Jr.
1st Lt. A.C. - 63rd Sqdn

'Upon bouncing a group of Me 109's I saw Lt. Daley clobber an Me 109 which immediately went out of control and crashed.'

Michael J. Jackson
Michael J. Jackson, 0440840
Capt., Air Corps.

HEADQUARTERS SIXTY SECOND FIGHTER SQUADRON

AAF Station F-150, APO 558
U.S. Army
Personal Combat Report
VIII Air Force F.O. No. 1451-A

Left:
Michael J. Jackson.

a. Combat (air)
b. 25 December 1944
c. 62nd Fighter Squadron
d. Approx. 1130 hours
e. Vicinity Bonn/Koblenz Area
f. Contrails persistent at 26/27,000'.
   Slight ground haze.
g. Me 109
h. One Me 109 claimed Destroyed.

i. I was leading Platform Squadron on a fighter sweep over the above mentioned area. After quite a bit of stooging, Nuthouse vectored us onto several groups of e/a. Prior to this my Blue Section lost me while investigating a bogie which turned out to be friendly. My Red and White Flights proceeded to climb above the e/a and I positioned the six of us on the 30 e/a which turned out to be Me 109's. On my initial bounce I pulled a little deflection on one Me 109 and got a few strikes. I continued to fire, closing to point blank range. The Me 109 then blew up and I had to pull up to avoid the pieces. We dispersed the entire group as they broke in every direction. I claim One Me 109 Destroyed.

Michael J. Jackson
Michael J. Jackson, 0440840
Capt., Air Corps.

Armament Report
Capt. Michael J. Jackson   44-19780   722 rounds API

'I was flying Capt. Jackson's wing when we went down to bounce the 25 plus Me 109's. On the first bounce I saw Capt. Jackson hit an e/a which blew up directly in front of me. I fired at two but am not sure whether I got any strikes.

Sanborn N Ball Jr
Sanborn N Ball, Jr., 0736069
1st Lt., Air Corps

Right:
Walter J. Sharbo.

HEADQUARTERS SIXTY SECOND FIGHTER SQUADRON

AAF Station F-150, APO 558
U.S. Army
Personal Combat Report
VIII Air Force F.O. No. 1451-A

a. Combat
b. 25 December 1944
c. 62nd Fighter Squadron
d. Approx. 1130 hours
e. Vicinity Bonn/Koblenz Area
f. Contrails persistent at 26/27,000'.
   Slight ground haze.
g. Me 109's
h. Two Me 109's claimed Destroyed.

i. I was flying No. Two in Platform Red Flight
when we sighted a gaggle of Me109's with fixed tail
wheels. We got into position for a bounce and Red Leader told us to pick our man and
go in. As I hit this first Me 109 he turned to the left, and my hits caused the plane
to go to pieces and glycol stream out. I believe the pilot was killed.
        An Me 109 got on my tail, and he turned with me and suddenly broke off. I
flipped over and saw another 109 in front of me. He was, I believe, the 3rd of (3)
three ships on Lt. Dailey's tail. I hit him in the cockpit and engine. Glycol poured
out and he slowly rolled to the right and went into a contrail vapour. When I came
thru on the other side he was on his side slowly going down. I believe this pilot was
also killed. I then rejoined with Capt. Jackson's flight.
I claim two Me 109's Destroyed.

Walter J. Sharbo
Walter J. Sharbo, T125496
F/O, Air Corps

Armament Report
F/O Walter J. Sharbo 42-28675   1,334 rounds API

(1st Plane) During this same air battle, I saw F/O Sharbo clobber one Me 109 which
also spun to earth in flames...

Michael J. Jackson
Michael J. Jackson, 0440840. Capt., Air Corps.

(2nd Plane) . . . Later I saw a P-47, believed to be F/O Sharbo, shoot down an Me 109
about 2000 yds. behind me. This e/a went straight down streaming smoke. One chute was
observed just after the bounce . . .

William C. Daley
William C. Daley, 0430790
1st Lt., Air Corps

SIXTY THIRD FIGHTER SQUADRON

Below:
Cameron M. Hart.

AAF Station F-150
APO 558
U.S. Army
Personal Combat Report
VIII Air Force F.O. No. 1451A
Captain Cameron M. Hart 0-803379

a. Combat
b. 25 December 1944
c. 63rd Fighter Squadron, 56th Fighter Group
d. 1150
e. SW of Cologne
f. CAVU
g. Me 109
h. One Me 109 Destroyed.

i. I was leading Daily Blue flight consisting of myself, Lts. Scherz, Andermatt and Clark. We were flying at about 26,000 feet SW of Cologne when I heard someone in Platform calling for help, and at the same time I saw several contrails going around about 5 miles SW of Cologne. I went over and immediately tagged on to an Me109. He split-s'd and I followed, catching up slowly. He pulled out after diving 5,000 feet and started to climb straight up. I started firing at about 600 yards, observing a few strikes and closed very rapidly on him, using water. At about 2-300 yards I saw strikes all over the 109 and it disintegrated in mid-air. I had to barrel-roll around him to avoid hitting the pieces. My oxygen was out or frozen, so I split-s'd for the deck and headed for home. I claim one Me 109 Destroyed

j. A/C No. 42-28810.
Ammo fired - 400 rds API.

Cameron M. Hart
Cameron M. Hart
Captain Air Corps

Supporting Statement
While flying Capt. Hart's wing, I saw a 109 below and in front of us. Capt Hart was closing rapidly when the 109 split-s'd, both of us following. On the pull-up, the leader (Capt. Hart) got many hits. The 109 was completely demolished in mid-air. I was unable to see Capt. Hart complete recovery due to an e/a on my tail.

Eugene W. Andermatt
Eugene W. Andermatt
2nd Lt., Air Corps

The sixth pilot to make a claim on 25 December 1944 was Samuel K. Batson. He had already claimed kills on 2 and 23 December. There appears to be no individual record of his claim on Christmas Day 1944, although his previous two combat reports do exist. Tragically Batson was killed a few days later, on 30 December 1944, and is buried at the Cambridge American Cemetery, Madingley, England.

Right: The grave of Samuel K. Batson at the American Cemetery, Madingley, Cambridge, England.

STEVE DARLOW

Name: Samuel K. Batson
Rank: Second Lieutenant, US Army Air Forces
Service No: O-714845
63rd Fighter Squadron, 56th Fighter Group
Entered the Service from: California
Died: 30 December 1944
Buried at: Plot D, Row 4, Grave 60
Cambridge American Cemetery, Cambridge, England
Awards: Air Medal with Oak Leaf Cluster

```
SIXTY THIRD FIGHTER SQUADRON

AAF Station F-150
APO 558
U.S. Army
Personal Combat Report
2nd Bomb Div. F.O. No. 533-B
2nd Lt. Samuel K. Batson

a. Combat
b. 2 December 1944
c. 63rd Fighter Squadron, 56th Fighter Group
d. 1310-1230
e. South of Merberg
f. Overcast
g. Me 109s
h. One Me 109 destroyed in air.

i. i. I was flying number 2 in Daily White flight on Major Conger's wing. We had just
let down through a thin layer of clouds when we observed twenty plus e/a flying south
at about 20,000 feet directly ahead of us, flying our type of formation. Not being
absolutely sure of their identity we closed behind them rapidly and identified them
as Me 109s with belly tanks. We lined up on a flight of four flying line abreast all
very close together and apparently unaware of our presence as they took no evasive
action. We had closed to within approximately 250 yards when I saw Major Conger open
fire on the two outside ships on the right. I saw strikes and large pieces flying off
of one of them, but didn't have time to observe any more as we were very close to them
and I was drawing a bead on the second ship from the left. I opened fire at about 200
yards, seeing strikes all over his canopy and several large pieces fly off his
fuselage. I then had to break off and pull up to avoid running into him as we were
right in top of them at this time. I glanced back over my shoulder and saw him roll
over on his back apparently very much out of control with black smoke pouring from
his airplane. I claim one Me 109 destroyed in air.

j. A/C No. 42-26658. Ammo. fired - 233 rds API
```

Samuel K. Batson
Samuel K. Batson
2nd Lt., Air Corps.

SIXTY THIRD FIGHTER SQUADRON

Below:
Samuel A .K. Batson.

AAF Station F-150
APO 558
U.S. Army
Personal Combat Report
VIII Air Force F.O. No. 1443A
2nd Lt. Samuel K. Batson

a. Combat
b. 23 December 1944
c. 63rd Fighter Squadron, 56th Fighter Group
d. 1145-1215
e. NW of Koblenz
f. CAVU
g. Fw 190
h. One FW 190 Destroyed.

i. I was flying Daily Red 2 on Lt. Trumble's wing with Lt. Daniel and Lt. Hoffman as number 3 and 4 men. We were at 27,000 feet NW of Koblenz when the group made contact with e/a and we were all ordered to drop our tanks. My leader then started orbiting to the left and we continued turning down to 18,000 feet, where there were many P-47s and Fw 190s making it very hard to distinguish friendly from enemy. We started an attack on a Fw 190 and he broke in my direction. I turned sharply to the left and was able to get behind him at a fairly long range. As I started to close he made a sharp climbing turn to the right, where at this point, I fixed him in my K-14 sight and began firing, the range being approximately 800 yards. He continued his climbing turn and I kept firing but did not observe any strikes until he had almost completed his turn, and I had closed to approximately 400 yards. I then saw strikes all over his airplane and his engine caught fire. I then broke off the attack and watched him go into a gentle spiral earthward, completely on fire by this time. I watched him go all the way down, hit the ground and explode, setting the surrounding woods on fire. I did not see the pilot bale out. I claim this FW 190 destroyed.

j. A/C No. 44-19960. Ammo. fired - 891 rds API

Samuel K. Batson
Samuel K. Batson
2nd Lt., Air Corps.

Supporting Statement
I was leading Daily Red flight with Lt. Batson on my wing. I was firing at a Fw 190 when another 190 came down on us from 9 o'clock and high. He overshot our flight and Lt. Batson opened fire on him. I saw many strikes on the e/a and it burst into flames.

Pershing B. Trumble
Pershing B. Trumble
1st Lt., Air Corps

With thanks to Buzz Took of the Halesworth (Holton) Airfield Station 365 Memorial Museum for help with this chapter (www.halesworthairfieldmuseum.org.uk). ■

Last Light at Gibraltar Farm. While the Battle of Britain was raging in 1940, a secret organisation was being set up in England to link up with resistance movements all over Europe. This 'Special Operations Executive' set about recruiting and infiltrating agents

and providing the resistance movements with the equipment to harass their German occupiers. The Royal Air Force played a key role in assisting the SOE to fulfil the orders of British Prime Minister Winston Churchill, to 'set Europe ablaze'. But there was a cost...

CHAPTER SIXTEEN

T HE AIRFIELD AT Tempsford, Bedfordshire, England, is best known as the wartime home of Royal Air Force No. 138 and No. 161 Squadrons. Throughout the second half of the war Whitleys, Halifaxes, Stirlings, Lysanders, and Hudsons had lifted from one of the Tempsford runways detailed for clandestine operations over occupied Europe, taking supplies to the Resistance, or infiltrating Special Operations Executive agents, including people like Violette Szabo and Wing Commander Yeo-Thomas, 'The White Rabbit'.

One evening, as the light was failing, I made a visit to 'Gibraltar Farm', the barn from which the agent's kit was issued prior to departure. It has now become a place of pilgrimage and commemoration for surviving veterans and the families of the men and women who lost their lives on the 'cloak and dagger' missions. Shadows were cast long, and a startled fox fled as I approached. It was a very still evening. Inside the barn, cobwebs and dust dulled the colouring of the numerous wreaths and crosses. Many of the gestures had been personalised; there was a human story behind each of them.

After some considerable time I went and sat at the end of the one remaining length of runway. Just as the sun dipped behind a bank of reddening cloud, a barn owl gently beat its way across the surrounding wheat field.

In the early hours of 1 June 1944 the No. 161 Squadron Hudson, piloted by 24-year-old Flight Lieutenant Warren Hale RCAF, was shot from the sky by flak, coming to earth near Gilze. The two Dutch agents, 2nd Lieutenant G. M. Dekkers and 2nd Lieutenant G. J. Kuenen, on board were killed, as were Hale and 20-year-old Flying Officer John Gall DFC RNZAF, and 32-year-old Flying Officer A. G. Maskall DFM. Flying Officer Michael Hughes survived, but attempts by his enemy to provide treatment failed, and he succumbed to his injuries. He is buried in Uden War Cemetery, while Hale, Gall, and Maskall rest in Bergen op Zoom Canadian Cemetery, Dekkers in Roosendaal Roman Catholic Cemetery, and Kuenen in Beverwijk (Duinrust) General Cemetery

At 1950 hours on the evening of 19 March 1943 No. 161 Squadron pilot Flying Officer Herbert Wynne DFM set out for Norway on Operation Vega 3 with his crew of seven, including 20-year-old Flying Officer Bill Franklin DFC. They were never seen again, and their names are engraved on the Runnymede Memorial.

On the night of 29/30 July 1942 Squadron Leader William Davies DFC took off from RAF Tempsford, in a No. 138 Squadron Whitley V, on Operation Lettuce 5. Over Holland a German night fighter shot the Whitley from the sky, and it plummeted to earth. White Commonwealth War Grave headstones now commemorate the final resting place of the entire crew at Holten General Cemetery.

Flak is assumed to have accounted for a No. 138 Squadron Stirling IV on the night of 26/7 February 1945. Detailed to take four agents to Norway, on operation Crupper 37, the aircraft plunged into the North Sea. The pilot, Flight Lieutenant Peter Cornwallis (Son of Sir Kinahan Cornwallis, G.C.M.G., C.B.E., D.S.O.), was one of four British nationals in the crew, along with two Australians and one Canadian. Their sacrifice is commemorated on the Runnymede Memorial.

TEMPSFORD AIRFIELD
GIBRALTAR FARM

ERECTED TO COMMEMORATE THE BRAVE DEEDS
OF THE MEN AND WOMEN OF EVERY NATIONALITY
WHO FLEW FROM THIS WARTIME AIRFIELD TO THE
FORCES OF THE RESISTANCE
IN FRANCE, NORWAY, HOLLAND,
AND OTHER COUNTRIES
DURING THE YEARS 1942 TO 1945

THE EQUIPMENT FOR THEIR DANGEROUS MISSIONS
WAS ISSUED TO THEM FROM THIS BARN

The night of 7/8 June 1944 was not a good one for No. 138 Squadron. The Halifax of Squadron Leader M. Brogan was written off following an accident on take-off, although there were no injuries. By the end of the night three further aircraft would be scrubbed from the squadron's strength. There was a total loss of life on the Halifax flown by 28-year-old Flight Lieutenant Herbert Jones RAAF, only one survivor from that flown by 20-year-old Pilot Officer Francis Lyne RCAF, and no survivors on Flight Sergeant Angus MacKay's RCAF Halifax. The twenty men who lost their lives, including 'Jack', were buried in French soil.

At 1920 hours on the night of 3 November 1943 Pilot Officer Henry Hodges hauled his No. 138 Squadron Halifax from the runway at RAF Tempsford. On board was Captain James Estes of the United States Army Air Force. By the end of the night seven of the eight men on board were dead, including James Estes. The one survivor, Sergeant Brough, managed to evade capture.

ACKNOWLEDGEMENTS

SOURCES

In addition to the people already mentioned at the end of chapters, our thanks extend to Chris Shores, Brian Mossemenear, Pete West, Steve Teasdale, Declan O'Flanagan, Steve Fraser, Rob Thornley, Steve Kitchener, Michael Lindley, Bob Yeoman, Gareth Jones and Associates, Richard Fusniak, Dave Clark, the Aldred Family, and Roger Audis for their help and support.

Most of the material published in *Fighting High* is based upon primary sources. However, the following secondary sources have also been consulted.

Chorley, W. R., *RAF Bomber Command Losses of the Second World War – 1939–1940* (Midland Publishing, 1992).
Chorley, W. R., *RAF Bomber Command Losses Volume 7: Operational Training Units 1940–1947* (Midland Publishing, 2002).
Chorley, W. R., *RAF Bomber Command Losses of the Second World War – 1942* (Midland Publishing, 1994).
Chorley, W. R., *RAF Bomber Command Losses of the Second World War – 1943* (Midland Publishing, 1996).
Chorley, W. R., *RAF Bomber Command Losses of the Second World War – 1944* (Midland Publishing, 1997).
Chorley, W. R., *RAF Bomber Command Losses of the Second World War – 1945* (Midland Publishing, 1998).
Middlebrook, M., *The Berlin Raids* (Penguin Books, 1990).
Shores, C., *Those Other Eagles: A Tribute to the British, Commonwealth and Free European Fighter Pilots who Claimed between Two and Four Victories in Aerial Combat, 1939–1982* (Grub Street, 2004).
Shores, C. and Williams, C., *Aces High: A Tribute to the Most Notable Fighter Pilots of the British and Commonwealth Forces in WWII* (Grub Street, 1994).
Wood, D. and Dempster, D., *The Narrow Margin* (Pen & Sword Military Classics, 2003).

INDEX

INDEX

Below:
The National
Memorial to the Allied
aircrew of the Battle
of Britain at
Capel-le-Ferne, near
Folkestone, Kent.

STEVE DARLOW